Stand Up –
Speak Up –
or Shut Up

Other books by L. Perry Wilbur:

How to Write Songs That Sell

Money in Your Mailbox

How to Write Books That Sell:
A Guide to Cashing in on the Booming Book Business

How to Write Articles That Sell

Stand Up - Speak Up - or Shut Up

A Practical Guide to Public Speaking

L. Perry Wilbur

Dembner Books • New York

Dembner Books
Published by Red Dembner Enterprises Corp., 1841 Broadway,
New York, N.Y. 10023
Distributed by W.W. Norton & Company, Inc., 500 Fifth Avenue,
New York, N.Y. 10110

Printed in the United States of America.

Library of Congress Cataloging in Publication Data
Wilbur, L. Perry.
Stand up, speak up, or shut up.
Includes index.
1. Public speaking. I. Title.
PN4121.W384 808.5′1 81-4387
ISBN 0-934878-05-6 AACR2

For my brother, Jack, a four-star communicator in and out of the courtroom and a real friend

Preface

The purpose of this book is to make you less shy about speaking in public, a more confident and skilled public speaker, and a better communicator in general.

It's truly a wonderful thing to be able to get up on your feet and speak to an audience. There is *power* in the spoken word, and this book will help you develop the skills to speak effectively — and to enjoy yourself in the process.

But a speaker must first pick the right subject, plan and write the speech, and decide how it can be presented to an audience most effectively. Along with a full discussion of these areas, the book highlights the four major types of speeches and gives examples of each.

Review points are included at the end of most chapters in the book. They are offered to make it easier for you to keep the key points of the chapters in mind, and will also serve as a quick reference in the future.

This book also covers all the complete tools of public speaking, including ways to identify with an audience, supprting materials for your speeches, the major methods of presenting a speech, gestures, keeping a speech on target, the use of examples and illustrations, showmanship, how to hook and retain an audience's attention (or regain it if it wanders), eye contact, handling the unexpected when speaking, suggestions for voice variety, using a tape-recorder, the beauty of pauses, sincerity, and more.

Some special features of the book are a comparison of the emotion used in speeches by Douglas MacArthur and John Kennedy, a recommended ideal way of speaking, an incredible story of how one woman became an inspiring speaker although starting out under great handicaps, a question-and-answer chapter, and specific help on planning and writing your speeches.

There are plenty of examples from a number of the world's great speeches and speakers. The last chapter offers twenty-nine ideas for speech projects, and these are broken down into areas of subject interest. In the back of the book you will find a handy checklist for more effective speaking and a self-scoring test to determine your potential as a public speaker.

This book will be your guide and road map to the fascinating and challenging world of public speaking. Refer to it often as you build your confidence and skill in speaking. There are lots of audiences out there waiting to hear what you have to say. May this book be a vital link between those audiences and the material you wish to communicate.

Contents

Stand Up—Speak Up—or Shut Up

1

The Ability to Speak Well Is Power

Ever stop to realize just how important speaking ability is to you in your life? What if someone waved a wand and you found yourself unable to utter any more words or sentences tomorrow? Your life would come to a silent halt.

The truth is that skill in speaking is power. It can bring you success, money, prestige, more satisfaction, much greater achievement during your life, and the interest plus plain fun of being a communicator.

The spoken word helps keep this old planet turning. Once you learn how to develop various kinds of speeches and present them with effectiveness and confidence, the world must take note of you.

Sigmund Freud summed up the great power of words very effectively: "Words have a magical power. They can bring either the greatest happiness or deepest despair; can transfer knowledge from teacher to student; words enable the orator to sway his audience and dictate its decisions. Words are capable of arousing the strongest emotions and prompting all men's actions."

A YOUNG PRESIDENT DESCRIBES THE NEW FRONTIER

Flashback to January 20, 1961. Inauguration day was a cold, snowy one in Washington. On the inaugural platform sat Dwight Eisenhower, who had been America's oldest president. Beside him was John Kennedy, who at forty-three was the youngest elected president.

A good idea of the hope, resolve, and vigor of John Kennedy was expressed in a particularly memorable statement from the inaugural address: "Let every nation know, whether it wishes us well or ill, that we shall pay any price, bear any burden, meet any hardship, support any friend, oppose any foe to assure the survival and the success of liberty."

It was almost at the end of his speech that Kennedy spoke one of the most famous and often quoted lines of his career: "Ask not what your country can do for you; ask what you can do for your country." Millions have long remembered him speaking these lines, with his hand jabbing the air to strengthen what he said. The lines, along with others, are carved in stone at Kennedy's grave site in Arlington National Cemetery. Kennedy obviously believed in a strong sense of loyalty and personal willingness to roll up one's sleeves and go to work for America. His famous quote reached many young people and sparked a greater feeling of patriotism in them.

WILLIAM JENNINGS BRYAN KNEW THE POWER OF THE SPOKEN WORD

William Jennings Bryan was a very popular speaker for some twenty-five years. His most famous address was the "Cross of Gold" speech, which he delivered before the Democratic convention at Chicago on July 8, 1896. There were twenty thousand people present.

Bryan had a strong talent for immediately grabbing an audience's attention and holding it throughout his speech. His voice, the way in which he led the audience, and his dramatic appeals all combined to make him a dynamic speaker. Here is the introduction of his "Cross of Gold" speech:

> I would be presumptuous, indeed, to present myself against the distinguished gentlemen to whom you have listened if this were a mere measuring of abilities; but this is not a contest between persons. The humblest citizen in all the land, when clad in the armor of a righteous cause, is stronger than all the hosts of error. I come to speak to you in defense of a cause as holy as the cause of liberty — the cause of humanity.

And here is the conclusion of that same speech:

> My friends, we declare that this nation is able to legislate for its own people on every question, without waiting for the aid or consent of any other nation on earth; and upon that issue we expect to carry every state in the Union. I shall not slander the inhabitants of that fair state of Massachusetts nor the inhabitants of the state of New York by saying that, when they are confronted with the proposition, they will declare that this nation is not able to attend to its own business. It is the issue of 1776 over again. Our ancestors, when but three millions in number, had the courage to declare their political independence of every other nation; shall we, their descendants, when we have grown to seventy millions, declare that we are less independent than our forefathers? No, my friends, that will never be the verdict of our people. Therefore we care not upon what lines the battle is fought. If they say bimetalism is good, but that we cannot have it until the other nations help us, we reply that, instead of having a gold standard because England has, we will restore bimetalism, and then let England have bimetalism because the United States has it. If they dare to come out in the open field and defend the gold standard as a good thing, we will fight them to the uttermost. Having behind us the producing masses of this nation and the world, supported by the commercial interests, the laboring interests, and the toilers everywhere, we will answer their demand for a gold standard by saying to them: You shall not press down upon the brow of labor this crown of thorns, you shall not crucify mankind upon a cross of gold.

Developing skill in speaking can bring more power to the following areas of your life:

1. Speech ability brings more power in your personal life.
2. Speech ability brings power in your school or college life.
3. Speech ability brings power in getting ahead in your job or career.
4. Speaking effectiveness brings power in business.
5. Speaking skill brings power in the professions.

MORE POWER IN YOUR PERSONAL LIFE

There was a boy in my high school speech class who had a real voice problem. He spoke with practically a soprano—almost a shrill voice. He was terribly ashamed of it and kept mostly to himself, as a result of it.

But a wonderful thing happened for this boy. His high school speech teacher took a special interest in his problem. She offered to help him with his speaking difficulty. He began staying after school and practicing the voice techniques she advised and explained to him.

As the months went by, his voice began to improve and grow less shrill and nasal. After a year, there was a remarkable difference. At the same time, his voice grew deeper and stronger, and his personal confidence developed, too. To sum up this true story, the boy became a fine speaker. He went on to college and landed many dramatic roles in plays. He acted on a weekly radio show for some five years. His whole life changed for the better.

He did graduate work at several universities and is today a highly respected college professor, as well as an expert on stage management and directing. The power that skill in speech brought into his life has continued through the years.

POWER IN YOUR SCHOOL – COLLEGE LIFE

Speaking ability also helps to overcome shyness. It's like swimming; the more you do the better you become at it. I remember a girl in the high school speech class I taught in Louisiana. She was very shy at first. But halfway through the school term, she seemed to find herself and her personality. Her speeches in class improved a lot. Her parents were very pleased with her development.

In my own case, speech training opened up a whole new world for me. One plus was the fact that it made me realize that there are good ideas for speeches everywhere. I had first taken speech in high school and liked it, so I made it my major subject interest in college.

The speech department of my college invited me to take part in the filming of a color documentary movie about the historic Shiloh battlefield some hundred miles east of Memphis, Tennessee.

I was one of ten actors in the film called *Shiloh: Portrait of a Battlefield.* The fields there are silent now. But after several days on location at the national park, the solemn atmosphere of the place got to me.

I listened in the evening breeze and could almost hear the sound of distant gunfire and booming cannon. Acting as an aide to General Grant in one scene, I walked the river road beside him, as he planned his strategy.

I saw trenches everywhere, listing the names of Union and Confederate states. The cannons, sitting silently in the fields, became etched in my mind.

As a confederate officer in a campfire scene, I huddled over a map, convinced throughout the scene that one of the restless horses beside us was going to kick me or all of the actors.

To this day, this award winning film is shown several times a week at the historic Shiloh National Park lodge.

My experience at Shiloh gave me some excellent material

for a speech about the battlefield and the experience of being in a film about the place. It also led me to write both an article and song about Shiloh. The article was published, and my song was later recorded and nationally released.

POWER IN BUSINESS AND THE PROFESSIONS

In the words of Clarence Randall, former Chairman of the Board of Inland Steel Corporation, "We are cut off from the public because we can neither write nor speak the English language with clarity and force." It seems clear that if a person can learn to be a better communicator, his or her business or professional career is bound to be more successful.

Gabriel Heatter was one of the Mutual Broadcasting System's most profitable and best known newscasters. He kept huge wartime audiences glued to their radio sets during the dark days of World War II. His deep baritone voice and famous, attractive opening line were unmistakable: "Ah, there's good news tonight."

Gabriel Heatter rose from the slums of New York to earn $400,000 a year for a considerable period of time. His initial reputation was made the night he melodramatically ad libbed, for forty-five minutes without a pause, the New Jersey state prison electrocution of Bruno Hauptmann—the kidnapper-murderer of the Lindbergh child.

Heatter's marathon coverage of the execution drew more than fifty thousand letters from listeners, stirring countless millions across America. This broadcast lifted him from the ranks of minor newsmen and turned him into a $3500 a week commentator. And that was a lot of money in those days.

Heatter developed the ability to pack a lot of information into his newscasts. Hs was very factual, but sometimes used semi-editorial interpolations in his reports. He would often broadcast from an unusual place, such as a coal mine or an airplane. These techniques helped to make him unique. He's well worth noting here, because he shows what can happen when you spot an opportunity and make the most of it. He was in the right place at the right time, but his style and unusual voice were what put him over, along with his marathon coverage of the electrocution.

Billy Graham has earned his place near the top of any list of dynamic communicators of the century. He's been criticized for playing on the emotions of his audiences. But there's no doubt that his compelling voice, style of delivery, variety of material, and excellent gestures combine to reach the majority of every large group that hears him speak. His speaking ability has made him the best known evangelist of the century.

More typical examples of people interested in improving their job or standing in the community — via speaking ability — include athletes, plumbers, doctors, salesmen, and secretaries. Housewives, too, can benefit from better speaking skills.

An athlete who can stand on his or her feet and speak with authority and conviction can be a useful spokesman for the school or university represented. Some schools and colleges send those of their athletes who have speaking ability on promotional tours, to interest new students in enrolling in that college or university.

More skill with the spoken word can improve a plumber's business relations with customers. Such plumbers can take a more active part in plumber associations.

Doctors who can speak effectively are sometimes invited to speak before annual meetings of the American Medical Association. They're also invited to address local, state, and regional medical organizations. As a medical authority, a doctor makes a fine guest speaker before various groups, and such appearances do much to make doctors well known.

Skill as a speaker can open up new club memberships for housewives. A housewife may wish to organize a special group of friends or neighbors herself. Confidence as a public speaker thus increases the enjoyment for a housewife and enables her to pursue more social, civic, charitable, and political interests.

When it comes to attending a business conference or convention, appreciation for and skill in speaking can pay off. The overall result is more effective communication. A great many businessmen take a visible part in the on-going work and advancement of their cities and surrounding areas. They raise funds, do charity work, promote worthy causes, stimulate the interests of youth, and sponsor a variety of meetings themselves. Better use of the spoken word is bound to help them . . . and enhance their reputations in the business community. People in business are sometimes asked by their superiors to present a report, speak to a department or branch of the company, or sell the features of some new proposal or venture. Being able to plan an effective oral presentation and deliver it is a definite stepping-stone to advancement in your business field.

STAGE FRIGHT — OR THE FEAR OF SPEAKING

Above all, don't let the fear of speaking — often known as stage fright — keep you from becoming a strong speaker. There are clear reasons for this fear. A great many people have it, so there's no reason to be ashamed about it. In fact, most speakers do better because of at least a small amount of nervousness. Some of the world's finest actors and communicators have admitted they get nervous, and claim that being keyed up helps them give a better performance.

Some basic reasons for too great a fear of speaking include the following:

- The fear of making a mistake and looking like a fool.
- The fear of just not measuring up in the eyes of those you know.
- The fear of getting up in front of strangers.

- The fear of your mind going blank—of forgetting what comes next in your speech.

Again, it's like swimming. The way to overcome your fear of it is to learn to swim. The same is true of speaking. You get over any fear of it by actually speaking before people. In time, you'll gain confidence that you can handle almost any speaking occasion. A little nervousness before you get up to speak is perfectly natural. Just don't worry about it. You'll usually do better because of it.

SIGNS OF POOR SPEAKERS

Some tell-tale signs of a fearful speaker can be seen in these examples:

1. *The speaker who bobs back and forth on his or her feet.* He or she may simply be a poor speaker, or just afraid. To avoid bobbing on your feet while speaking, plant both feet on the floor with not too much space between them. Check at different times during your speech, so you're certain that both feet are on the floor and that you don't appear to be bobbing back and forth.
2. *The speaker who goes from one "and . . . ah" to another all the way through the speech.* You can eliminate this trap by careful rehearsal of your speech. Taping your speech on a recorder and listening to it will reveal whether you're guilty of this fault. Knowing your speech well is the best insurance against too many "and . . . ahs."
3. *The speaker who can't slow down.* The words come out at a mile a minute. Have a friend or member of your family listen to your speech. Ask them to pay special attention to your rate of delivery. It takes some effort, and requires going over your speech time and again to correct an overly fast delivery, but it's well worth it. Much of your

speech will be missed by the audience if it's presented at too rapid a rate.

4. *The speaker who presents the material at too slow a rate.* Talking too slowly will also drive your audience to distraction. Remember, you don't have an unlimited time period in which to give your speech. Too slow a rate will take too long, and many people in your audience will become bored and will tune you out. Strive for a moderate rate of delivery.
5. *The speaker who has no variety, pauses, or gestures.* The best way to insure that *your* speech has good variety and an appropriate number of pauses and gestures is to plan your speech with them in mind, and then double-check them when recording your speech. Strive not to say everything in the same way. Your voice, for example, can be low in some spots and louder or more forceful in other places. Work out a number of gestures you plan to use well in advance. If you do this and then practice your speech enough, you'll know automatically when and where to use each gesture.

How do you know how far you can go as a speaker and communicator unless you try? A college coach helped actor Karl Malden go into acting, by refusing to let him act in a school play. Malden went on to carve a highly successful career of playing character roles on the stage and screen. He won an Academy Award for his 1951 best supporting actor performance in *A Streetcar Named Desire.*

You'll learn in this book that you can certainly be a more effective communicator. You'll see positive examples of quality communication, and you'll find out how to plan and organize a speech and the nature of the major kinds of speeches. You'll be guided on how to develop into a speaker who not only has something to say but who also says it well.

During the dark days of World War II, Winston Churchill was visiting a school classroom. It was thought that he meant to say something cheerful to the students. But the thought of the

Germans and what they were doing to England so enraged him that he suddenly slammed his cane over an empty desk and shouted to the startled students: "Never give up. Never never never never never give up."

I say to you not to give up on the idea and goal that you can become a more confident and effective public speaker. You'll find the way in this book.

REVIEW POINTS FOR POWERFUL SPEAKING

- Skill in speaking is power. It can bring you more achievement, prestige, and satisfaction.
- The speech of William Jennings Bryan known as the "Cross of Gold" address was so powerful in its effect that Bryan was nominated for president the next day.
- Effectiveness as a speaker can literallly change your life for the better.
- Speaking ability helps to overcome shyness.
- A great many people have a fear of speaking in public. The truth is that most speakers do better because of at least a small amount of nervousness.

2

You Can Communicate More Effectively

By striving to improve your skills in your use of the spoken word, you can certainly upgrade your total communication effectiveness. Increased skill with the spoken word will also help you to be able to write better.

In recent years, news reports have revealed that an increasing number of schools are turning back to the basics of speaking, writing, reading, and math. There's a definite trend today for more attention on basic speaking skills.

The desire and basic human need to express youself is a strong one. Lots of people go through their lives communicating very little, or only when they have to, simply because they don't feel comfortable or confident as communicators. Many of them never really learned the art and skill of good communication. But there's no reason why any individual has to settle for poor communication ability. Improvement can and does come with effort and practice.

According to William Brigance, a respected authority on speech communication: "Mere ideas do not make a speech." A speaker needs to organize these ideas, to put them in logical sequence, and support them with facts or stories or anecdotes. The speech should hang together with a beginning, middle, and end.

Whatever method you choose to present your speech, some kind of solid, written framework for the material is necessary. It may consist of an outline, extensive notes, or a full manuscript. The important thing is to plan and build the structure for your speech, as a basic preparation for presenting it. Whatever the delivery method may be (extemporaneous, outline, notes, memory alone, or full manuscript), more skill with the written word will produce a better speech.

Speaking and writing actually have the same basic purpose. This purpose is to transmit or communicate thought and emotion from one person to another or others. Speakers, of course, address an audience. But writers do the same thing. There's an audience of readers who will be reading what a writer has to communicate. And both use words as the method of communication. So there are strong similarities between speaking and writing.

EVERYTHING STARTS WITH GOOD COMMUNICATION

Whether it's a business, a radio or television station, the council group of a city which plans its future, a network, a branch of the military service, a family (couple and children), or a key department of the government, *everything* starts with good communication. The quality, or lack of it, in the organization can often be traced back to its type of communication. Not many organizations can grow or progress if there's a communication breakdown.

In his excellent book, *The Process of Communication*, David Berlo states that "there's a real purpose in communicating: the words we can command, and the way we put them together affect what we think about, how we think, and whether we are thinking at all."

Man has continually resorted to war to solve problems. Now that we have the power to destroy our whole race, we clearly need a better way to deal with problems on this planet. We must learn to use skillful communication to resolve conflicts and disagreements by peaceful means. Speaking and writing will continue to be two of the major ways to transfer thoughts, attitudes, knowledge, and opinion. History, itself, is the recorded chronicle of man's sojourn on this planet. If man can learn to express himself better in speaking (as well as writing), he can hopefully draw nearer to truths, and thus realize more freedom and happiness.

HOW *YOU* CAN BECOME A BETTER COMMUNICATOR

There's a tried and proven way in which you can improve your skills as a communicator. As a former college teacher of courses in Communication, I assure you that this method works. It helped most of the students in my classes, along with an adult class I also taught. Both students and adults from all walks of life can use this method with good results. Some of my students even realized, through this method, that the communications field was the right vocation, the right place, for them.

Here's a summary of my proven method to make you a better communicator. It consists of two basic steps:

1. Buy yourself a fairly thick notebook or record book. Start at once to write down, or list, what *you* feel are good examples of communication. In other words, as you go about your daily routine and wherever you are on weekends, start collecting any and all examples of what YOU believe amounts to good or bad communication.
2. The second step is to consult your growing list frequently and think about what you've written down as good or bad communication.

After a few weeks or months, your list of communication examples will have grown considerably. The items you list can come from anywhere. Such examples might well cover many of the following:

1. Radio-television commercials you feel represent good or bad communication
2. Newspaper editorials
3. Cartoons
4. Magazine articles
5. Newspaper feature stories
6. A record or album (music can communicate, too)
7. A photo or painting you saw somewhere
8. A billboard message
9. Print advertisements from some publication
10. The key idea in a speech or address you heard or read
11. Humor in its variety of forms
12. Greeting cards (they communicate well and use a minimum number of words to do it)
13. Ideas from books or novels
14. Comedy routine ideas
15. Various other sources

When you start collecting and keeping your list, be sure to write down *the reason why* you selected each example. Just tell briefly in your own words why you feel that each item is an example of good or bad communication. Your comments might range from something like "good use of emotional appeal" to "reveals how the artful use of humor can cut through ice."

By recording the reasons you selected each example of communication, you can easily review your list at a later time, and you'll be reminded why you chose each item. One of the examples in your list, for example, might look something like this:

5. Coffee commercial on television network show—It was poor communication because, as a whole, it seemed to insult the viewer's intelligence.

You can, of course, say more than the above example if you wish. But the basic idea is to cite your example of communication from whatever source and then tell why you feel it was a good, bad, or mediocre example.

Believe me! If you start and maintain such a list for preferably three, six months, or longer, you're *bound* to learn more about communication. Why? Simply because you're observing and noting what you feel are good and bad examples from all areas of the messages being beamed at you. You will thus become more sensitive in time to what strikes you as good quality or poor quality communication. You will be much more conscious of the wide varieties of possible examples, too.

Becoming a more skilled and effective communicator involves more than keeping a list of examples. Such a list helps to make you more aware of the material and ideas being directed at you every day. Read over your list frequently (once a week at least), along with the reasons you put down for choosing each example.

This second step includes some of the basic things you can do to actually improve your speaking. Some of these ideas will interest or appeal to you more than others. You probably will think of techniques you might want to try. Here are some action pointers that have helped many others. To improve as a speaker, you can do the following:

1. Read some of the *great* speeches by famous speakers (Lincoln, Churchill, Bryan, Daniel Webster, and so on). This will get you familiar with the great orators of the past.
2. Listen to recordings of some of the world's finest speakers and voices. There is much inspiration to be gained in this way.
3. Attend lectures and addresses by the many speakers who visit your city or town. Take a notebook with you

and criticize them on paper. As you listen to them speak, try to determine how they could have done better.

4. Practice speaking with a tape-recorder. Even thirty minutes or an hour a day can work wonders in your speaking ability. Take notes when you play the tape back and then work to improve.
5. Think about signing up for a course in Speech Communication (often called Basic Speech or Public Speaking) at the nearest college or university in your area.
6. Offer to teach any kind of class for youth or adults. A skill you may have or previous background-training might qualify you to teach a class. This front line teaching will require you to speak and communicate more every day.
7. When you feel that you've gained enough confidence and have improved your speaking, offer to speak anywhere and everywhere — free. The experience will be invaluable for you.

As you think about upgrading your speaking ability, and actually follow through on some of the above suggestions, you'll be able to add ideas of your own that seem especially right for you.

Remember, if you really want to develop skill and power as a speaker, and possibly go places with it, you can certainly do just that. It will take some time and effort, but you'll definitely see the results if you stay with it. Some of the chapters to come in this book will guide you on the way to becoming a much better speaker, who has something to say and knows how to get it across most effectively.

REVIEW POINTS FOR POWERFUL SPEAKING

- You can do a lot on your own to upgrade your speaking ability.

- An increasing number of schools are placing more attention today on speaking skills.
- Many people go through life communicating very little, because they don't feel confident or comfortable as communicators.
- Ideas alone do not make a speech. The ideas must be organized. The ability to prepare an outline for a speech or a manuscript is important too.
- The basic purpose of both speaking and writing is to transmit (communicate) thought and emotion from one person to another or others.
- Collecting examples of good and bad communication develops knowledge and makes you more sensitive to the ideas and messages being beamed at you almost constantly.

3

Finding the Best Subjects for Your Speeches

An old saying in the world of public speaking holds that "there are two kinds of speakers: those who have something to say and those who have to say something." While this general rule has almost become a cliché, there is still much truth in it.

There is of course a real difference in having something solid to say and just having to say something. The former idea means that you're interested in the subject. The latter means that you have to get up and say something (just to get through with it).

Whenever you choose a subject for a speech, and throughout the planning and presentation of your speech, keep one clear-cut goal constantly in mind: the objective of every speech is to keep an audience interested enough so they will listen to the entire presentation.

Here are some useful steps in finding good subjects for a speech. Refer to them whenever you're faced with selecting a suitable subject:

1. Ask yourself what subjects stimulate and are of interest to you. The answers you get will suggest a number of possible subjects. Be sure to also ask yourself what you might like to say about a subject you like.

2. Ask yourself if the subjects that interest you can be made interesting to your audience.
3. List any broad subject areas you already know something about, because of previous training or special knowledge you have. Then see if you can narrow the overall subject down to a specific part. Here are some examples:

Broad Subject Area	*Central Idea*
Politics	the large amount of money needed to run for office
Investing	why real estate is the best investment of all
Travel	shorter, more freqent trips are growing more popular

4. Once you have a number of central ideas for speeches (meaning the subjects reduced to a specific area of interest), look them over carefully. A few of them will stand out as the ones you would prefer to develop into full speeches.

   You might wish to use the star rating method, which is the technique I use. This is quite simple and helps to determine the quality of various speech subjects or central ideas. I've used the star system for years, as follows:

   **** A four-star subject for a speech means the central idea behind it is excellent.
   *** A three-star idea means the idea is good.
   ** Two stars denote an average idea for a speech. I think of two stars as fair.
   * One star is used to indicate a poor idea, but sometimes such ideas can be upgraded into a two or three-star idea.

5. The next step is to select the one subject to go with (central idea) from those you like. To make this decision, consider each of these factors:
   What type of people will be in the audience listening to your speech . . . and is this subject (your narrowed central idea of that subject) right for them?
   Does your chosen subject seem likely to hold the attention and interest of this particular audience?
   Will the time and place where you present your speech influence the subject? (Sometimes national or world-wide events can make a certain speech topic more relevant, interesting, helpful, or entertaining.

WHERE TO FIND GOOD SUBJECTS FOR YOUR SPEECHES

Here is a list of sources for possible speech subjects. You'll find it helpful to run down this list, when you want to consider the possibilities open to you. Keep in mind that how good a subject turns out to be often depends on how well the material for it is handled. Some subjects for speeches are, of course, better than others. What you seek is the *best* subjects for you. Various factors already cited will also have an influence on your choice of subject and central idea. The time and place of your speech, the interest areas, age, education level, and general background of your audience, length of the speech, and other factors must all be considered.

Here are some useful sources of subjects for speeches:

1. Your Daily Newspaper—There's a goldmine of good speech subjects in newspapers, whether they're small or large, from cities or rural areas. Overseas newspapers are also loaded with good ideas. Whenever you spot a likely subject, or specific central idea for a speech, cut it out and file it for future reference.

2. Magazines—Any and all kinds of magazines are a natural source of up-to-date speech subjects. And don't forget about the vast array of magazines published in Canada, England, Australia, Japan, and other countries.
3. Radio-Television—Good subjects for speeches are often suggested by something you may hear or see on radio or television. A speech I heard on "Grooming and Training a Poodle" was sparked by a television news item. So stay alert for ideas. A television interview I watched led me to an excellent idea for a speech on Shiloh National Park, site of one of the most awesome battles of the Civil War.
4. Remarks by and conversations with family, friends, and relatives—A chance remark by a family member, or conversation with a friend, can lead you to original and well-focused subjects (central ideas) for speeches.
5. Books—All manner of books, from the past and the present, are loaded with ideas for speeches. In many cases, you can find the specific, central ideas for any number of speeches in books. It's well worth noting this source as one of the best ones.
6. Your own personal experience—When you get right down to it, *you're* the most interesting person in the world, certainly to yourself. So don't forget your own past experience as a rich source of possible speech ideas. Your former jobs, schools, travel,military service, and so on are just a few obvious examples.
7. Other speeches you hear or read—Hearing or reading other speeches may well influence you to choose a certain subject for a speech. Don't fail to take advantage of the chance to hear local speakers in your area.

If you attend any kind of annual conference, seminar, or convention, you'll be hearing a number of speakers. Why not take some notes and think about related subjects or central ideas for a speech? After hearing psychic Jeanne

Dixon speak in Washington, D.C., a few years ago, I got the idea for a speech about the ability to predict the future. It turned out to be one of my most effective speeches.

While these sources usually offer the best opportunities for finding an inviting speech subject, other possibilities include newsletters, pamphlets, bulletins, business reports, advertisements, songs, and even signs or posters. Indeed, ideas for good speeches are practically everywhere, once you are alert to them.

HOW TO SELECT DYNAMIC SPEECH SUBJECTS

Many people feel that choosing a subject for a speech — the right subject — is perhaps the most important aspect of public speaking. Naturally it is important, but planning the speech and presenting it well are crucial too. Since you often have a number of possibilities to consider, choosing a subject is usually the most difficult aspect of the art of speech-giving (though many others feel that actually presenting the speech is the hardest part).

So to help you do well in selecting the right subjects, I'm listing below some twenty *specific desires* wanted by most people everywhere. I urge you to strive to pick subjects that are related or tied in with one or more of these universal wants. Why? Simply because your audience will be much more interested and attracted to your speech, if it ties in with some of the desires shared by most of the human family. Here are the twenty universal desires. Refer to them when you're thinking about a subject for a speech. Remember, the more of these human wants your speech subject is related to, the better and more effective your speech will be:

- To have security
- To be appreciated
- To have beautiful possessions
- To be popular

- To enjoy oneself
- To be healthy
- To be clean
- To attract the opposite sex
- To save time
- To escape physical pain
- To make money
- To be praised
- To satisy one's appetite
- To be in style
- To take advantage of opportunities
- To be creative
- To be successful
- To gratify curiosity
- To be self-confident
- To have more leisure time

TESTING YOUR SPEECH SUBJECTS

In addition to relating your subject to at least some of the universal wants, you need to consider these steps to test the subject you're thinking about:

1. Does the subject (or central idea of the speech) keep popping into your head over a period of time? If so, that could be a clue that it's a right subject for you.
2. If you get ideas on how you could develop the central idea (of the subject) into a full-length speech, this may be a sign of a good subject choice.
3. If you're torn between two or more subjects, think about which one you could treat in an original way. It's the *way* you treat the subject—the angle of focus you and your experience bring to it—which is important. So don't worry if your overall subject choice seems trite or overused. How YOU treat or handle it will make all the difference.

It's usually wise to avoid certain types of speech subjects. You should generally avoid a subject that is too technical or involved. Some examples include "How to Fly an Airplane," "Operating Today's Modern Computer," statistical subjects, or other subjects which are just too difficult. Try not to use subjects which are over the heads of most audiences.

Seek also to avoid any subject you consider to be below the intellectual level of those who will hear your speech. Be sure that their background and education match up with your focused speech subject. This will help to insure that your speech is well received.

SPEECH SUBJECTS TO STIMULATE YOUR THINKING

What follows is a list of general subjects for all kinds of speeches. I believe that you'll find it useful to run down this list of topics whenever you seek a suitable subject for a speech. Any one or more of these can set up a train of thought and lead you to decide on a suitable subject. These topics are meant to stimulate your interest and also show you the wide variety of choices open to you for a speech subject. Some of them are more focused than others:

1. "Theater Is Magic"
2. "How Washington Wastes Tax Dollars"
3. "England: The Last Civilized Nation"
4. "The Meaning of Real Friendship"
5. "Walt Disney: The Master Creator"
6. "The Death of America's Downtown Areas"
7. "Dangers of the Persian Gulf"
8. "The Tinderbox of the Middle East"
9. "The Loyalty of Pets"
10. "Whatever Happened to Courtesy?"
11. "Country Music Is Big Business"
12. "Modern Movies"
13. "The Good and the Bad of Jogging"

14. "Shiloh: Portrait of a Battlefield"
15. "Grooming and Training a Poodle"
16. "The Satisfaction of Achievement"
17. "Era of the Psychic"
18. "Let's Make America Great Again"
19. "Traveling in Europe Today"
20. "The Shrinking Value of College Degrees"

REVIEW POINTS FOR POWERFUL SPEAKING

- There are two kinds of speakers: those who have something to say and those who have to say something.
- The objective of every speech is to keep an audience interested enough so they will listen to the entire presentation.
- When you have a speech subject in mind, see if you can narrow it down to a specific area of interest called the central idea.
- A one to four star rating system is useful in deciding on the quality of various speech ideas.
- The more you know about your audience, the more likely you'll be able to plan and present an effective speech.

4

Planning and Writing Your Speech

Once you're convinced that you have something to say, via your choice of speech subject and the central idea of it, you're ready to start planning and writing your speech.

It's an excellent idea at this point to try to state the premise or major purpose of your speech. One way that has worked well for many speakers over the years is to sum up the thrust of the speech in one important *purpose sentence.* In other words, put the purpose of your speech into a key sentence. A purpose sentence, in effect, puts the central idea of your speech into one basic statement. With a purpose sentence to refer back to, while planning and writing your speech, you are much more likely to know where you want to go. Then check your speech, as it develops, to be sure it's continuing in the right direction.

You'll also find it very helpful to include (in your purpose sentence) what kind of response you seek from your audience. Do you want to inform them, entertain, persuade-convince, or perhaps inspire them? Ask yourself how you hope your speech will change them, and your answer will let you know the general response desired.

Some students who are required to speak in a speech course wait until the night before the day of their speech to decide what they're going to say. The same is true for a number of adults. They often wait far too long to decide on the subject, content, and ingredients of their speeches. The usual results of such delays are poor speeches and a waste of the audience's time and attention.

THE PARTS OF A SPEECH

Once you know the subject, central idea of your speech, purpose sentence, and overall response you seek from the audience, it's time to start planning the introduction, middle part, and ending of your speech. Here is an example of the way a speech may evolve:

> *Subject* — Money.
> *Central idea* — To tell the audience how to build a second income (building a second income).
> *Purpose sentence* — To inform the audience on the most practical ways to build a supplementary income.
> *Desired audience response* — To teach the audience how to add to their yearly income, and to motivate them to put one or more plans into action.
> *Introduction* — Use quotes and shocking statements on today's galloping inflation. Explain the need for a side or extra income.
> *Middle part of speech* — Present the main points on how a second income can be realized. Back up the main points with supporting materials.
> *Conclusion of speech* — End with either a summary of the main points or an effective anecdote illustration on the value and importance of an extra source of money in today's modern era.

A strong speech will have all three essential parts (beginning or introduction, middle part, and ending). The introduction is the most important of the three, because without an attention-getting opening, you will lose most of your audience. An audience won't stick around to hear the middle part (or body) of your speech, or the ending, if you haven't presented an effective introduction.

PLANNING THE INTRODUCTION

You have a choice in planning the introduction. You can decide on two or three points to be made in the body of the speech, after writing out a purpose sentence. Or you can plan an introduction *first,* before thinking about what major points to include in your speech.

A sound rule of thumb is that most introductions for speeches count for about ten percent of the total speech. When you're planning an introduction, consider the following guidelines:

- The introduction of a speech puts the spotlight on the subject.
- The introduction tells the audience why they should listen. It offers promise of a worthwhile speech to come.
- Above all, the introduction of a speech grabs the attention-interest of the audience and makes them want to listen.

The introduction for a speech may include a variety of tools, all designed to attract attention and make an audience want to stay with you, as the speaker, instead of tuning out. Here are some of the most useful tools. You can use any one of them alone, or several of them in combination:

A strong quotation related to the subject of your speech

EXAMPLE: Franklin Roosevelt's call to the American people (December 29, 1940, in Washington) to make the United States "the arsenal of democracy."

> The Nazi masters of Germany have made it clear that they intend

> not only to dominate all life and thought in their own country, but also to embrace the whole of Europe, and then to use the resources of Europe to dominate the rest of the world.
>
> It was only three weeks ago their leader stated this: "There are two worlds that stand opposed to each other." And then in defiant reply to his opponents he said this: "Others are correct when they say: 'With this world we cannot ever reconcile ourselves.' I can beat any other power in the world." So said the leader of the Nazis.

EXAMPLE: A speech by Harry Emerson Fosdick

> One ought to read with awe these words spoken nearly two thousand years ago and only now beginning to seem obviously true. Reliance on violence is suicidal, said Jesus. "All they that take the sword shall perish with the sword."

An unusual statement or remark used by a speaker to open the speech

EXAMPLE: An address by Billy Sunday

> The trouble with many men is that they have got just enough religion to make them miserable. If there is not joy in religion, you have got a leak in your religion. Some haven't religion enough to pay their debts.

A narrative description of an amusing or dramatic happening

EXAMPLE: Lincoln's Gettysburg Address

> Fourscore and seven years ago our fathers brought forth on this continent a new nation, conceived in liberty and dedicated to the proposition that all men are created equal. Now we are engaged in a great civil war, testing whether that nation, or any nation so conceived and so dedicated, can long endure.

The use of one or a series of curious questions

EXAMPLE: A speech on patriotism by Emma Goldman

> What is patriotism? Is it love of one's birthplace, the place of childhood's recollections and hopes, dreams, and aspirations? Is it

the place where, in childlike naivete, we would watch the floating clouds, and wonder why we, too, could not run so swiftly? In short, is it love for the spot, every inch representing dear and precious recollections of a happy, joyous and playful childhood?

A series of remarks meant to present a preview of the speech to follow

EXAMPLE: Theodore Roosevelt's speech to the Hamilton Club in Chicago, in 1899

> Gentlemen: In speaking to you, men of the greatest city of the west, men of the state which gave to the country Lincoln and Grant, men who preeminently and distinctly embody all that is most American in the American character, I wish to preach not the doctrine of ignoble ease but the doctrine of the strenuous life; the life of toil and effort; of labor and strife; to preach that highest form of success which comes not to the man who desires mere easy peace but to the man who does not shrink from danger, from hardship, or from bitter toil, and who out of these wins the splendid ultimate triumph.

The use of a vivid comparison, which has direct bearing on the speech and leads up to it

EXAMPLE: Reverend Martin Luther King Jr.'s "I Have a Dream" speech

> Five score years ago, a great American, in whose symbolic shadow we stand today, signed the Emancipation Proclamation. This momentous decree came as a great beacon of light and hope to millions of Negro slaves who had been seared in the flames of withering injustice. It came as the joyous daybreak to end the long night of captivity. But one hundred years later, the Negro still is not free.

A compliment paid to the audience. This can work well, but it should be an honest compliment

EXAMPLE: Mrs. Franklin Roosevelt's speech about the United

Nations (before the Democratic National Convention in Chicago, 1952)

> You are very kind to me and I am glad to have been asked to talk to you about the United Nations, about its past, about what it is doing today and more important, about its future.

An observation on the occasion for the speech or reason for it
EXAMPLE: Susan B. Anthony's speech (1873) "Are Women Persons?"

> Friends and fellow-citizens: I stand before you tonight under indictment for the alleged crime of having voted at the last Presidential election, without having a lawful right to vote. It shall be my work this evening to prove to you that in thus voting, I not only committed no crime, but, instead, simply exercised my citizen's rights, guaranteed to me and all United States citizens by the National Constitution, beyond the power of any state to deny.

The telling of an interesting anecdote, if it has a connection with the speech
EXAMPLE: Cornelia Otis Skinner's speech at Lake Placid (June, 1953) before the convention of the American Gynecological Society

> Ladies and gentlemen of the profession. . . . if not the oldest in the world, at least one of the most time-honored. You find me in a more awkward position than any in which I have ever been placed by certain of your distinguished members. In fact I feel as uncertain of the issue as I did on an occasion when, giving a monologue performance a number of years ago in a New England town, I started off under the handicap of a far from encouraging introduction. The lady of the organization which was . . . having me . . . rose and with fluttering apology said "Ladies and gentlemen, owing to the high price of Rear Admiral Byrd, we have Miss Skinner with us this evening." Well, let's face it . . . you have Miss Skinner with you this evening and its not owing to the high price of any of the fees you have charged me over the years.

A statement (often witty) used by the speaker to identify with the audience and let them know that the subject of the speech will have interest for them

EXAMPLE: Mark Twain's speech at the annual dinner of the New England Society (December 22, 1876)

> Gentlemen: I reverently believe that the Maker who made us all, makes everything in New England — but the weather. I don't know who makes that, but I think it must be raw apprentices in the Weather Clerk's factory, who experiment and learn how in New England for board and clothes, and then are promoted to make weather for countries that require a good article and will take their custom elsewhere if they don't get it. There is a sumptuous variety about the New England weather that compels the stranger's admiration — and regret.

EXAMPLES OF INTRODUCTIONS TO SPEECHES

SPEAKER: "I'm very honored by your invitation to speak to your group tonight." (You then go on to commend the group for its work or accomplishments and lead into the subject of the speech.)

SPEAKER: (on the subject of creative achievement) "Her husband, a handsome young pianist, had died shortly after they were married. Ruth, a young girl from Toronto, Canada, was left to face the future alone. The piano her husband had loved so much now remained closed. She had loved it, too, because of him. But now she kept it closed, so it wouldn't remind her so much of him. One night this grief-stricken young Canadian decided to re-channel her grief into music, by trying to compose a song." (This introduction really got attention.)

SPEAKER: (Flashback type of introduction) "It was a day of witchcraft trials. No matter who you were, suspicions that you might well be a witch were the talk of the town or village. It was a dangerous time. Your next-door neighbor might be jailed at any moment on the very same charge. Nobody trusted anyone or knew what to believe."

SPEAKER: (Religious-inspirational speech) "Can the finite know the Infinite? Perhaps partially. But no human being can ever really fully comprehend the vastness, unlimited energy, and incredible power of the Infinite. And yet—small and insignificant as we may sometimes feel—each one of us is a part of this enormous power. Each person is much like a stitch in the great tapestry being woven by God."

THE MIDDLE PART OF YOUR SPEECH

The body or middle part of a speech consists of the main points which you wish to highlight, backed up by supporting materials for each of those key points. There are two steps in planning the main points for your speech:

1. Decide what your major points will be.
2. Arrange them in the most effective order, from the view of your audience.

After you have your main points set, your next step is to select the supporting materials for each major point. The supporting materials, used to lend weight and credibility for each major point in a speech, include illustrations, specific examples, facts or figures, quotations by authorities or experts on the subject, and comparisons.

In other words, an effective middle part of a speech has major points supported with evidence. You don't proceed from one main point to another post haste; you back up each one of your points with ammunition as to why that particular point should be believed or accepted by the audience.

It makes sense, then, for you to do some advance thinking and planning, when considering a given speech subject and the central idea behind it. If you can get an early idea of what your main points will consist of, and how you can support each one of them, you'll have a much better sense of direction for your speech, and a good start toward making it a success.

A good case can be made for waiting to plan your introduction, until after you have your main points and supporting materials lined up. After you see what the body or middle section of your speech is going to consist of, you can plan a stronger introduction. In fact, some of your main points may provide clues for a good introduction.

SUPPORTING MATERIALS AND IDEAS

Remember, your presentation of the main points of your speech, plus the supporting materials used for each one, will form the middle part, or body of your speech. Refer to the following supporting materials and ideas, when you're planning the middle section of your speech:

- Illustrations
- Testimony (quotes from authorities and experts)
- Description
- Contrast and comparison
- Factual material (facts, figures, and statistics)
- Anecdotes and specific instances
- Narration

EXAMPLE OF ILLUSTRATION (from Harry Emerson Fosdick's "A Christian Conscience About War")

> Nevertheless, at the same time that this nationalistic process has been going on, another movement has been gathering headway. The enlarging fellowship of human life upon this planet, which

> began with the clan and tribe and moved out through ever widening circles of communication and contact, has now become explicitly and overwhelmingly international, and it never can be crowded back again.

EXAMPLE OF TESTIMONY (from Emma Goldman's speech on "Patriotism — a Menace to Liberty")

> What, then, is patriotism? "Patriotism, sir, is the last resort of scoundrels," said Dr. Johnson. Leo Tolstoy, the greatest antipatriot of our time, defines patriotism as the principle that will justify the training of wholesale murderers."

EXAMPLE OF DESCRIPTION (from Mark Twain's speech about the New England weather)

> Now, as to the size of the weather in New England — lengthways, I mean. It is utterly disproportioned to the size of that little country. Half the time, when it is packed as full as it can stick, you will see that New England weather sticking out beyond the edges and projecting around hundreds and hundreds of miles over the neighboring States. She can't hold a tenth part of her weather. You can see cracks all about, where she has strained herself trying to do it.

EXAMPLE OF CONTRAST AND COMPARISON (from Theodore Roosevelt's speech on the "doctrine of the strenuous life")

> These are the men who fear the strenuous life, who fear the only national life which is really worth leading. They believe in that cloistered life which saps the hardy virtues in a nation, as it saps them in the individual; or else they are wedded to that base spirit of gain and greed which recognizes in commercialism the be-all and end-all of national life, instead of realizing that, though an indispensable element, it is after all but one of the many elements that go to make up true national greatness. No country can long endure if its foundations are not laid deep in the material prosperity which comes from thrift, from business energy and enterprise, from hard unsparing effort in the fields of industrial

activity; but neither was any nation ever yet truly great if it relied upon material prosperity alone.

EXAMPLE OF FACTUAL MATERIAL (facts, figures, and statistics) from Harry E. Fosdick's speech before the League of Nations Assembly Service (September, 1925)

> The old appeals for war in the name of a good cause fall coldly now on the instructed ear and cease to carry conviction to thoughtful minds. "Would you not go to war to protect the weak?" men ask. The answer seems obvious. A modern war to protect the weak—that is a grim jest. See how modern war protects the weak: 10 million known dead soldiers; 3 million presumed dead soldiers; 13 million dead civilians; 20 million wounded, 3 million prisoners; 9 million war orphans; 5 million war widows; 10 million refugees. What can we mean—modern war protecting the weak? The conviction grows clear in increasing multitudes of minds that modern war is no way to protect the weak.

EXAMPLE OF ANECDOTES AND SPECIFIC INSTANCES (from a speech-sermon by Billy Sunday)

> Out in Iowa a fellow came to me and spread a napkin on the platform—a napkin as big as a tablecloth. He said, "I want a lot of shavings and sawdust."
>
> "What for?"
>
> "I'll tell you: I want enough to make a sofa pillow. Right here is where I knelt down and was converted, and my wife and four children, and my neighbors. I would like to have enough to make a sofa pillow to have something in the house to help me talk to God. I don't want to forget God, or that I was saved. Can you give me enough?"
>
> I said: "Yes indeed, and if you want to make a mattress, all right, take it; and if you want enough of that tent to make a pair of breeches for all the boys, why take your scissors and cut it right out, if it will help you to keep your mind on God."

EXAMPLE OF NARRATION (from the "Cross of Gold" speech by William Jennings Bryan)

> You come to us and tell us that the great cities are in favor of the gold standard; we reply that the great cities rest upon our broad and fertile prairies. Burn down your cities and leave our farms, and your cities will spring up again as if by magic; but destroy our farms and the grass will grow in the streets of every city in the country.

THE CONCLUSION OF YOUR SPEECH

Your objective in concluding a speech is to bring your presentation to a satisfying ending. A great many speakers accomplish this by offering their audiences some type of summary, or wrap-up, of what has been said.

Here are the main ways in which to conclude a speech, with examples of each method:

A summary or wrap-up of what you've already said in the speech.

EXAMPLE (from Theodore Roosevelts's "Doctrine of the Strenuous Life" speech)

> I preach to you, then, my countrymen, that our country calls not for the life of ease, but for the life of strenuous endeavor. The twentieth century looms before us big with the fate of many nations. If we stand idly by, if we seek merely swollen, slothful ease, and ignoble peace, if we shrink from the hard contests where men must win at hazard of their lives and at the risk of all they hold dear, then the bolder and stronger peoples will pass us by and will win for themselves the domination of the world. Let us therefore boldly face the life of strife, resolute to do our duty well and manfully; resolute to uphold righteousness by deed and by word; resolute to be both honest and brave, to serve high ideals, yet to use practical methods. Above all, let us shrink from no strife, moral

or physical, within or without the nation, provided we are certain that the strife is justified; for it is only through strife, through hard and dangerous endeavor, that we shall ultimately win the goal of true national greatness.

A tying together of the main ideas of your speech, by means of quotation.
EXAMPLE (from John F. Kennedy's address to the General Assembly of the United Nations on September 22, 1963)

> Two years ago I told this body that the United States had proposed, and was willing to sign, a limited test-ban treaty. Today that treaty has been signed. It will not secure freedom for all. But it can be a lever; and Archimedes, in explaining the principles of the lever, was said to have declared to his friends: "Give me a place where I can stand, and I shall move the world."
>
> My fellow inhabitants of this planet, let us take our stand here in this Assembly of Nations. And let us see if we, in our time, can move the world to a just and lasting peace.

A looking-ahead-to-the-future type of ending.
EXAMPLE (from Reverend Martin Luther King Jr.'s "I Have a Dream" speech)

> I have a dream that one day every valley shall be exalted: every hill and mountain shall be made low, the rough places will be made plane, the crooked places will be made straight and the glory of the Lord shall be revealed and all flesh shall see it together.
>
> This is our hope. This is the faith that I go back to the south with. With this faith, we will be able to hew out of the mountains of despair a stone of hope. With this faith, we will be able to transform the jangling discord of our nation into a beautiful symphony of brotherhood. With this faith, we will be able to work together; to play together; to struggle together; to go to jail together; to stand up for freedom together knowing that we will be free one day.

A conclusion which leaves your audience with a challenge or appeal to action.
EXAMPLE (from Patrick Henry's "Liberty or Death" speech)

> It is in vain, sir, to extenuate the matter. Gentlemen may cry peace, peace— but there is no peace. The war is actually begun! The next gale that sweeps from the north will bring to our ears the clash of resounding arms! Our brethren are already in the field! Why stand we here idle? What is it that gentlemen wish? What would they have? Is life so dear, or peace so sweet, as to be purchased at the price of chains and slavery? Forbid it, Almighty God! I know not what course others may take; but as for me, give me liberty, or give me death!

A polishing up on the main thoughts or gist of your speech.
EXAMPLE (from Lincoln's "Gettysburg Address")

> It is rather for us to be here dedicated to the great task remaining before us— that from these honored dead we take increased devotion to that cause for which they gave the last full measure of devotion— that we here highly resolve that these dead shall not have died in vain— that this nation, under God, shall have a new birth of freedom— and that government of the people, by the people, for the people, shall not perish from the earth.

The use of an effective illustration or anecdote.
EXAMPLE (from Mrs. Franklin Roosevelt's speech on the United Nations)

> In World War Two when I visited so many hospitals in the Pacific, I was glad I had traveled so much through my own country and could say to a loney boy far from home: "You come from Lubbock, Texas?" The boy's face would light up. "Yes ma'am. I remember when you were there." I can only hope that in the future there may be some little unexpected values which will come out of these latest travels too.
>
> I hope all our travelers may serve the great common hope that through the United Nations peace may come to the world.

When you're involved in planning your conclusion for a speech, you'll find it helpful to see if you can sum up your total speech in one sentence. Such a key sentence will aid you in seeing a number of ways to arrive at a logical and satisfying ending.

OUTLINING A SPEECH

You may not wish to use a formal outline, when planning and writing a speech. If not, just decide on and work out the introduction, middle part, and ending, but three divisions of a speech are an outline in themselves (even if not an elaborate one).

Here are some examples of speech outlines. They may give you ideas for your own outlines.

Title of Speech: "Man's Amazing Ability to Predict the Future"
Outline of Speech:

I. Introduction (stating evidence that this ability to predict the future exists)

II. Main points of speech backed with supporting materials. Main points include:

   A. The importance of accuracy in predicting the future. (Contrast the predictions of gypsies and professional psychics.)
   B. The growth of interest in prophecy. (Give facts on prophecy as a business.)
   C. The mind is more than we know. (Cite experiments in ESP at both Duke University and Stanford.)
   D. The Titanic. (Tell dreams of people with loved ones aboard the ship and the premonitions involved.)
   E. Track records of famous psychics. (Actually cite some of their predictions which came true).

III. Conclusion. (Cite conclusions based on research and

opinions of experts. Include the use of guesswork in arriving at various predictions.)

Title of Speech: "Imagination Can Change Your Life"
Outline of Speech:

I. Introduction. (Open with anecdote on how the human imagination is like a genie in a lamp.)

II. Main points of speech backed with supporting materials:
  A. Increased imagination can take you places.
    1. Cite illustration of Thomas Mitchell, the actor, and how he moved into show business.
    2. Jules Verne's incredible use of imagination
    3. "Whatever the mind of man can conceive can become reality."
  B. Imagination in the business world and marketplace
    1. Cite the way an imaginative Ohio insurance agent sells.
    2. Imagination in advertising, marketing, and promoting products and services
  C. How to develop more imagination
    1. Give opinions from experts and authorities on increasing imagination.
    2. The importance of reading more
    3. Mind association and the game of *What if?*
  D. The right ideas for you
    1. Quantity versus quality
    2. The case of Thomas Edison
    3. Recognizing good ideas for you
  E. Imagination in action
    1. The amazing Walt Disney
    2. Dorothy Kilgallen's round-the-world publicity trip
    3. Roy Huggins: Creator of "The Fugitive"

III. Conclusion (Use illustration-anecdote from the film "Miracle on 34th Street," where Kris Kringle describes the wonders of the imagination for a little girl named Susan.

I urge you to do an outline for each of your speeches. There are other ways to plan a speech besides an outline, but I've found the use of one very helpful in my own speaking. Many fine speakers would never think of planning, much less writing a speech, without first doing an outline.

Here are some of the sound reasons for doing an outline:

- A speech outline gives you a track to run on. You know where you're headed.
- A speech outline creates confidence and enthusiasm. You derive a better feeling about your overall speech.
- An outline gives structure and unity to your speech.
- With an outline, you're less likely to leave out some important ideas or material.
- An outline gives you a plan for the presentation of your speech. You're therefore able to see on paper how your speech will develop. The outline serves as a beacon of light.

HOW LONG WILL YOUR SPEECH BE?

The decision on length for a speech depends on a number of factors including the following:

1. For what occasion is the speech being presented? Is it a holiday speech, political rally, commemorative occasion (a speech honoring a certain person or observing a particular historical event), or what?
2. What kind of audience will hear the speech? Is it a group of students, a women's club, a group of businessmen, a civic club, religious gathering, patriotic, or what? It also helps a

speaker to know about the background of the audience (age level, educational history, interests).

3. Where will the speech be presented? Will it be given in a large auditorium, a classroom, assembly hall, club house, hotel banquet room, rural schoolhouse, church meeting-room, or where?

Other factors may also have an influence on the length of a speech: conditions such as the time of a speech, how warm or cold it is in the hall or room where the speech is heard, the noise level (airplanes going over, heavy traffic) and platform facilities.

It's generally wise to see that your speech doesn't run too long. Most speeches tend to run about twenty to thirty minutes. Some lecture programs may run forty-five minutes or more, if a question-and-answer period follows the presentation.

WRITING YOUR SPEECH

It's very possible to write what you think is a wonderful speech on paper and realize later, after its presentation, that your material failed to achieve your desired purpose. In other words, stay ever aware that what looks good on paper (when you write your speech) may not get across to your audience.

As you write your speech, strive to use shorter, more down-to-earth words. Try to get sentences that communicate. Oral material is different from the written form, in the sense that a speech is meant to be heard by an audience. Consider the following:

Good speaking	*Good writing*
1.Same material as in good writing, but short sentences. Action verbs.	1.Examples of parenthetical phrases, asides, long sentences, many clauses.
2."Representative government needs to hear dissent in	2."Spring is a great time to be alive. Each time spring re-

the state . . . needs to be aware of the views of the people. You (the people) are the ones who determine how the government will function." (from a speech by Senator Howard Baker) This was good speaking, because it is clear, direct, and right to the point.

turns, she comes laden with precious gifts; warm sunshine on your back, fields of wild flowers, lingering twilight that somehow is even more delightful at the close of a spring day, gentle breezes that caress you soft as a melody. Yes. Spring is tender. She is sweet. She is a lover." (The descriptive phrases help make this good writing.)

3. "Discipline in action? There are plenty of examples of it. How about mountain climbers? They certainly need a strong amount of discipline to both train for their climbs and to actually reach the summits of the mountains they scale. Mountain climbing is a dangerous sport. Even the best known climbers have to be alert and on their guard constantly, in order to prevent accidents. A high amount of discipline and expert training are musts for those climbing teams that reach summit after summit." (This is good speaking, because of the clear illustration presented on *discipline in action.)*

3. "One of us has to go; man or the automobile. With more than 60,000 Americans losing their lives in motor accidents every year, it's obvious that present safety measures are not doing the job. While there are a number of standard causes for auto accidents, such as drunken driving, one cause is seldom discussed or even mentioned: Rudeness. It's doing more than its share of the killing on the roads." (The is good writing, because it presents facts in an interesting way. The sentences invite further reading.)

4. "But we have given you a far healthier world than we found. Rickets and worms, which once afflicted one-third of the south, are rare. You need no longer fear epidemics of flu, typhus, typhoid, smallpox, scarlet fever. Some of you have probably never seen a goiter. Childbirth is no longer feared." (This is good writing, because of the short sentences and series of supporting points made for the premise of the speech.)

4. "I wanted to meet Jeanne Dixon very much, so after about a fifteeen minute wait, I managed to get my crowd-weary six-feet frame up to the front. I shook hands with her and told her how much I'd enjoyed hearing her. She gave me one of the little white cards, which she gives to well-wishers and those she meets. I saw the famous psychic, who has the signs of the gift of prophecy in her own hand, take the hand of a small girl. Jeanne told the little girl that she had good vibrations, and that she would grow up to do some great things in the field of art." (This is good writing, because it gives the reader a "you-are-there" feeling. The anecdote is both revealing and interesting.)

Remember, your listeners have only what they hear to go on. They will not see or read your speech. You want words, ideas, and sentences which can be readily transmitted to an audience. Strive to speak in images and in pictorial ways. Use shorter, more simple sentences in your speeches. Avoid parenthetical phrases or asides. Tell stories in sequence.

USEFUL TIPS ON WRITING YOUR SPEECH

When you're ready to write out your speech, the following guidelines will prove to be useful and practical. They are based on proven principles and a number of written speeches:

1. Get down the material of your speech in double or triplespace. This will give you room for corrections and changes. And it will help in learning your speech.
2. Write down all the main thoughts and ideas of your speech.
3. Be sure the order of your speech moves from a strong introduction to a middle part (with two to five main points, followed by supporting materials), and on to a satisfying conclusion.
4. As you write your speech, stop and read aloud various sections of the material. Better still, tape record and listen to sections over and over. Imagine the words and sentences being heard by an audience. Ask yourself at all times if each point in your speech will get across to your audience.
5. Use words that say what you mean, not complicated, long, and technical sounding terms.
6. Short sentences for the most part will make your speech more effective. In President Franklin Roosevelt's December 8, 1941 declaration of war speech, he made a skillful use of short and right-to-the-point sentences: "Last night Japanese forces attacked Hongkong." "This morning the Japanese attacked Midway Island."
7. A good case can be made for doing several drafts of your speech manuscript. Then you can go over each one, thinking about the ideas and lines themselves and asking yourself if each one is what you really wish to say.

REVIEW POINTS FOR POWERFUL SPEAKING

- Try to sum up the overall thrust of your speech in one key purpose sentence.
- Know in advance what your speech objective is. Do you want to inform your audience, entertain them, persuade, or inspire?
- Three main divisions of a speech are the introduction, middle part, and the conclusion.
- The introduction of a speech must grab the attention and interest of the audience.
- The middle part of a speech consists of the main points (no more than five), backed up by supporting materials (illustrations, quotes, contrast, visual aids).
- Many speeches conclude with a summary or wrap-up of what has been said.
- An outline is a great help in planning a speech. It gives you a track to run on.
- A written manuscript for a speech is no assurance that communication will take place. The material must be lifted from the page and transmitted to an audience in an effective manner.

5

The Speech to Inform

One of the major types of speeches is the all-important speech to inform. Audiences the world over gain new information on a wide variety of subjects, via this kind of speech. Many of the speeches you may present in the future will fall into this category.

To inform an audience in a speech is to transmit or communicate certain information and facts about a particular subject. Consider the following:

- To inform is to clarify. To inform an audience, you must clarify the facts or information which you have selected for your speech.
- To inform is to explain what something means, tell how a certain process works, how an event took place, or the way in which something is used.

Here is an example from a speech to inform on how to be more creative:

> Experiment. Be on the lookout for those ideas that seem to leap out at you . . . those ideas that are right for YOU. Some people experiment with ideas in their minds while commuting to work, or on a lunch break, or at coffee, or while waiting in line somewhere. Keep in mind that all of these are good times for you to be working on an idea. For all I know, you could be developing some creative

idea even now. Whenever you work on an idea, stay with it. The more you think about an idea, the more suggestions or possibilities will come to your mind for that idea. Use the association method with your ideas. Ask what is it related to? Let your mind wander. Play with an idea, nurse it along. It might take care of you some day. It may grow into a giant that could change your life.

WILL THE AUDIENCE LEARN FROM YOUR SPEECH?

Aside from the general truth that it's possible to learn from a variety of different speakers, the speech to inform should reflect this learning purpose (or instructional-informational purpose) to a considerable degree. Whenever you plan a speech to inform, ask yourself the following questions:

1. What do I want my audience to learn from my speech?
2. What is the *best way* to transmit this learning? What are the main points I must get across, plus sub-points, so this objective can be achieved?
3. What supporting materials (examples, illustrations, quotations by experts and authorities) can I use to back up this learning goal?

The answers to such questions will be a real aid to you, in the planning and development of your speech. Your audience will hear your speech but once. You must therefore strive to be well prepared to fulfill your purpose for this speech, which is to inform your audience and help them to derive a genuine sense of having learned something about the subject.

SOME EXAMPLES OF THE SPEECH TO INFORM

In a recent speech given by Britain's Margaret Thatcher (delivered at the Lord Mayor's Banquet in London), the topic was "The West: In Good Shape to Face International Upheavals."

Here are some of the key ways her speech achieved its purpose of *informing* the audience:

1. Her speech informed the audience about the international prospects for the next few years.
2. Her speech *communicated* information regarding the uncertain era the west is in (at this time of writing).
3. Margaret Thatcher made it clear that military clashes and political upheavals will continue to take place in critical parts of the world (but that the west is in good condition to meet them).
4. Her speech also highlighted the ways in which Britain can lead and help the west, due to the qualifications of experience and tradition.

"How the Truth Became a Lie (The Need for Honor in Public Discourse)" was a speech given a few months ago by Joseph E. Reid, president and chief executive officer of Superior Oil Company. The speech was given at the Management Night Program of the Houston Association of Petroleum Landmen. Notice how the introduction of the speech appeals to the audience's curiosity:
Introduction: "You and I have heard it all already. The energy crisis . . . the need for domestic energy supplies . . . Open government bureaucracy, and on and on. We've heard it all. We know it too well. We've told it to each other in places like this, and we've listened to others tell it."

Reid wanted his audience to know how our language is being manipulated today and how the truth has become lost between the lines. He informed his audience in the following ways:

1. With the use of a disturbing question, Reid revealed to the audience that America doesn't know what is true. ("The nation cries out. What is true?")

2. Reid informed the audience that something is happening to our language . . . that it's being corrupted.
3. Reid made it clear that our society has begun to lose the means of identifying, recognizing and telling the *truth*. He backed this up (supporting material) with a review of the key national events of the past twenty years including Watergate, Billygate, and Koreagate.

Reid's major speech purpose was to inform, but it also had elements in it of the speech to persuade. Speeches that deal with planning in one way or the other are meant to inform. Here are some examples:

1. "Planning for the Future of Memphis" (given by a city administrative officer)
2. "New Year's Resolutions I Wish I Could Keep"
3. "Plan Your Work and Work Your Plan"
4. "Planning Where You'll be in 1995"
5. "Ten Master Secrets of Planning"

DON'T GET TOO TECHNICAL

If you want to keep your audience with you, in the course of your speech, strive not to get too complicated or technical. Some statistics and details may of course be necessary in certain speeches, but avoid overdoing it. Even a minister speaking to a church congregation can quickly lose a chunk of the audience-congregation by getting bogged down in a mass of complicated figures and facts. I've seen this happen any number of times, while hearing a number of sermons.

Try your best instead to sum up what a mass of technical figures *mean*. Sum up their underlying meaning for your audience. Do advance work for your audience. They want to feel that you've done your homework, as leader and interpreter of all facts and figures, and most of your audience will want to follow you. But don't overload them with too many involved points.

IDEAS FOR A SPEECH TO INFORM

Most or all of the speeches you may be asked to present in the future (or will choose to present) may well have this basic purpose: informing the audience. So remember that it's one of the most important kinds of speeches.

The occasion on which you give a speech may of course also have a bearing on the type of material you select. For your future reference, here are some basic ideas for a speech to inform. Feel free to use any of them for actual speeches of your own:

1. "How to Get More Out of Your Leisure Time"
2. "Is the Sky Really the Limit for Today's Graduates?"
3. "Picking Up the Pieces After Iran"
4. "Second Thoughts About Jogging" (This one would also include persuasive elements.)
5. "The Shrinking Value of College Degrees"
6. "How to Handle Youself in Job Interviews"
7. "Brainstorming Can Solve Your Problems"
8. "Coping With the Battle of the Bulge"
9. "You Can Change the World"
10. "Let's Make America Great Again"

REVIEW POINTS FOR POWERFUL SPEAKING

- One of the major types of speeches is the speech to inform.
- Your audience will hear your speech but once. You must therefore strive to be well prepared to fulfill your purpose, which is to inform your audience . . . and to provide instructional or informational material.

- The speech to inform may also have elements of the speech to persuade, inspire, and entertain.
- It's best not to overload your audience with too many technical or complicated points.

6

The Speech to Persuade

The ability to persuade via the spoken word is real power. The art of persuasion is one of the true marvels of life. It keeps nations moving forward, cities growing, and human lives achieving. Take away persuasion and thousands of products and services would stop being sold. In addressing an audience, the speech to persuade is one of the most important of them all.

Candidates for president and other offices rise or fall, depending on their basic ability to persuade people to vote for them. Company advertising campaigns succeed or fail, according to how well they motivate consumers to buy a particular product or service. As Helen Woodward says in her book, *It's an Art,* "The best ads aren't the ones about which you say, 'Isn't that clever?' but the ones which make you take out your pocketbook and buy something." And that means persuasion.

Adolf Hitler knew the power of oral persuasion and used it to the hilt for his destructive purposes. Others have, of course, used it for good. Men like Benjamin Franklin, John Adams, Thomas Jefferson, Abraham Lincoln, Franklin Roosevelt, John Kennedy, Winston Churchill, and many others made effective use of persuasive communication via the spoken word. In so doing, they lifted the horizons of mankind and made the world a better place.

Never forget this vital truth about oral persuasion. It has the potential power to *sway the masses*. The gift of oratory is an awesome one, when developed enough, and used with intelligence and wisdom by those who have the skill.

TOOLS OF THE PERSUASIVE SPEECH

Aristotle, who wrote a master work on persuasion and rhetoric, said that "the use of a persuasive speech is to lead to decisions."

The belief and conviction of some members of an audience are rather easy to change by a skilled speaker. But others in every audience may be much more difficult to sway. To persuade those holding mildly held beliefs, you simply need to have a solid number of logical and sound reasons why the listeners should change their opinions. When the beliefs held are very strong, however, you will need all the persuasive power you can bring to bear on the matter. This means evidence, and lots of it, in the form of facts, statements and quotes by noted experts or authorities in the field, examples, illustrations, statistics, and all the supporting ammunition you can muster. The majority of persuasive speeches are meant to stimulate attitudes of listeners. Here are some of the most useful tools you can use to persuade an audience:

1. Strong use of facts and evidence as to why the audience should change its belief
2. Testimony and the opinions, views, and statements of known authorities
3. Clear and specific examples
4. Comparisons
5. The presentation of all persuasive ideas (of the speech) in a meaningful way

When planning your speech to persuade, it's a good idea to decide exactly what you seek to persuade your audience about. Then determine in advance how you intend to go about accomplishing it. Ask yourself how they can be persuaded. What kinds of evidence will be most useful to you? This type of speech takes careful planning and outlining. One of the first things you must decide in this type of speech is how to get the audience to not only accept you, as speaker, but also to *believe* what you say.

So you have to win over your audience soon, and the best way to do it is through some kind of identification. When planning and outlining your speech to persuade, ask yourself these questions:

- How can I identify myself with my audience? There are clues for doing this in the background, interests, and common goals which you share with your audience.
- What appeals or motivating influences can you cite, in order to reach your audience (such as patriotism or nationalism, family and home appeals, and religious or political appeals)?

EXAMPLES OF IDENTIFYING WITH AN AUDIENCE

SPEAKER: "I grew up in this state and still think of it as my second home."

SPEAKER: "The American way of life, as we know and love it, is threatened today."

SPEAKER: "While this is my first opportunity to visit in England, I have long been concerned about the welfare and future of your nation."

OUTLINING YOUR SPEECH TO PERSUADE

The following steps will result in an effective and persuasive speech, assuming that you can present or communicate the material in a forceful and compelling way:

1. Write out a clear basic sentence stating exactly what it is

you'll be asking the audience to do. What is it you want to persuade them to do (to give money, to support a cause, cast a vote, change an opinion, understand a different view, or perhaps to take action on some matter)?

2. Decide on your introduction for the speech. You need an especially strong opening or hook in order to grab attention. An appealing title will help.
3. Determine and collect the strongest evidence you can obtain for backing up the reasons why your audience should make a change in their attitude, opinion, or whatever. Know your evidence well and know where you will use it in your speech. (Use many examples, testimony, quotes, comparisons, illustrations, statistics, and facts.)
4. Find a way to identify with your audience, so they will tend to accept and believe what you say.
5. Write out the introduction.
6. Plan and write out the main points to be covered in the body (or middle part) of your speech.
7. Plan and write out the conclusion. Remember, you can summarize your main points, use a strong story, example, or illustration that wraps up the gist of your speech, or just bring it to a logical ending.

HOW TO KEEP YOUR SPEECH ON THE TARGET

Good eye contact with your audience is even more important in the speech to persuade. Your audience will be judging how much *you* seem to be convinced, yourself, of what you're saying.

The order in which you present the main points and ideas of your speech will have a bearing on how well it's received. Discuss the most significant points first, moving on down to the less important ones.

Aristotle claimed that the only essential parts of a speech

are (1) the statements and (2) the argument. Generally speaking, a forceful style of delivery by you, the speaker, can help persuade your audience. Persuasion is more difficult to achieve than informing or entertaining an audience. So I especially urge you to tape-record your speech to persuade (and preferably every speech you plan to present) and then listen to it, making notes on how you can imporve the overall effect of your total speech. Aristotle emphasized that effective persuasion must:

1. Work on the emotions of the audience
2. Give the right impression of the speaker's character
3. Prove the truth of the statements made

Never lose sight of the major goal of your speech, which is to persuade the audience to accept what you're saying, and believe it, thus possibly changing either a mildly or subbornly held view or opinion. Or your objective may be to lead the audience to take some form of action.

Your style of delivery, use of clear words, skillful blending of short and long sentences, the overall way you handle all the material of your speech, your choice and use of motivating appeals, how well you succeed in exciting the listener's emotions, and repetition of important facts or evidence will all determine whether or not real persuasion takes place.

EXAMPLES OF PERSUASIVE SPEAKERS

Any list of persuasive speakers would have to include Ronald Reagan, Ted Kennedy, Winston Churchill, Paul Harvey, Howard Baker, Phyllis Schlafly, John Kennedy, Eleanor Roosevelt, Adlai Stevenson, Barry Goldwater, Billy Graham, Oral Roberts, Harry Truman, Edward Murrow, and Eric Severeid (just to name a few).

What follows are parts of some persuasive speeches. They have been selected to show examples of the important parts of

such speeches and the techniques of speakers:
Introduction of Franklin Roosevelts's first inaugural address (March 4, 1933). The morale of the nation at that time was very low. Banks were closing and unemployment was great.

> First of all, let me assert my firm belief that the only thing we have to fear is fear itself — nameless, unreasoning, unjustified terror which paralyzes needed efforts to convert retreat into advance. In every dark hour of our national life a leadership of frankness and vigor has met with that understanding and support of the people themselves which is essential to victory. I am convinced that you will again give that support to leadership in these critical days.

Example of the middle part of a speech (also from Franklin Roosevelt's first inaugural address):

> Our greatest primary task is to put people to work. This is no unsolvable problem if we face it wisely and courageously. It can be accomplished in part by direct recruiting by the government itself, treating the task as we would treat the emergency of a war, but at the same time, through this employment, accomplishing greatly needed projects to stimulate and reorganize the use of our natural resources.

Notice how Roosevelt's words were not only persuasive and assuring; they communicated a new spirit of hope to the people across America. His inaugural speech seemed designed to signal that a better era had arrived, a new beginning for the nation.
Example of an analogy-comparison used in the conclusion of a persuasive speech by Billy Graham:

> A worm is perfectly helpless. It has no strength to fight or protect itself from danger. Whether food for birds or to be trampled underfoot by man, it resigns itself to sacrifice; but the worm is always busy. Hidden away out of sight, it gets little credit for what it does, yet it is the greatest blessing to plant life in the world. It lives

entirely for others. A worm is of the earth earthly but it plows its way through the darkness, it feeds and thrives and grows fat on the very earth that brings such trials and headaches to others.

I beg of you, Christians, learn the lesson of the worm and humble yourself before God.

SUGGESTED IDEAS FOR A SPEECH TO PERSUADE

In case you're stumped for a speech to persuade, here are some suggestions for this type of speech. Most of them are meant to stimulate the audience to action or to change-enforce a belief or opinion held by the audience:

1. "Wake Up, America" (to persuade the audience to be more vigilant and patriotic)
2. "Your Brain Improves With Use" (to persuade the audience to support and take an active part in continuing education)
3. "Children Are Children for Just a Little While" (to persuade an audience to make the most of their short time and chance to influence children)
4. "St. Jude's Hospital: Symbol of Hope" (to persuade the audience to contribute to and support the work of the well-known children's hospital in Memphis, Tennessee)
5. "Prayer Changes Things" (to persuade the audience that a regular prayer life does make a real difference)
6. "Teaching Deserves Your Best" (to persuade an audience composed mostly of teachers to give only their best to the profession)
7. "The Case for Talking Things Out" (to persuade the audience of the value and benefits of discussing issues and problems, instead of remaining silent)

Refer back to this chapter whenever you plan to present a speech to persuade. And keep the following definition of persuasion in mind, as left to us by Saint Augustine: "A person is persuaded if he or she likes what you promise, fears what you say is imminent, hates what you censure, embraces what you command."

Remember. Another word for persuasion—especially today—is power. If you can persuade, you can usually write your own ticket. The more persuasive you can become, the greater your success is likely to be.

REVIEW POINTS FOR POWERFUL SPEAKING

- The art of persuasion keeps nations moving forward, cities growing, and human lives achieving.
- Oral persuasion can sway the masses. Ronald Reagan did evidently convince millions of the need to make America great again and to make Washington, D.C., once again "a shining city on a hill."
- Some members of an audience are rather easy to persuade. Others may be difficult to influence, because of strongly held or stubborn beliefs, opinions, or views.
- The speech to persuade requires careful planning and outlining.
- The background, interests, education, and common goals which you may share with your audience can be of help in seeking ways to identify with your listeners.
- Your audience will be judging, especially in a speech to persuade, just how much *you* seem to be convinced of what you're saying.

7

The Speech to Inspire

Another clear reason or purpose for speaking to an audience is to inspire them. Parts of this type of speech may also inform, persuade, or entertain, but the main objective of the speaker in this kind of speech is to uplift and inspire the audience.

Inspiration may have any of the following effects on listeners (or a combination of them):

- The listener feels "on fire" about something.
- The listener feels that "all is not lost," "life can be and often is beautiful," "the best is yet to be" or whatever.
- The listener feels an influence to make his or her life count more. A change in the listener's basic attitude takes place.
- An idea, viewpoint, subject, or theory is cast in such a light, or communicated in such an ennobled way (by you, the speaker) that the listener comes away with a fresh, vivid, and possibly exciting new perspective.

EXAMPLES OF INSPIRATION IN ACTION

> Now the trumpet summons us again—not as a call to bear arms, though arms we need; not as a call to battle, though embattled we are; but a call to bear the burden of a long twilight struggle, year in and year out, rejoicing in hope, patient in tribula-

tion; a struggle against the common enemies of man: tyranny, poverty, disease and war itself.

— John Kennedy's inaugural address
on January 20, 1961

A good friend of mine once let me in on his secret of never letting anything get him down in spirit. As the Creative Director of a large advertising company, Bud's daily routine was rugged. Yet he faced problems, setbacks, and all manner of troubles with enthusiasm and a powerful assurance that everything would work out okay.

It usually did. Everyone was amazed at his dynamic, positive outlook. One day, after he had been through a particularly hectic conference, I cornered him in his office hoping to find out how he did it. I've never forgotten what he said that day: "Whenever I feel low or things go wrong, I read some inspiring material or listen to an inspiring speaker. It may be a magazine, a book, or a speaker, but I always find the right word for me at the time."

(from a study on creativity)

The famous story of the birdman of Alcatraz is a memorable example. In prison for life, this amazing man went all the way with his interest in birds. He became a recognized expert on bird diseases and their treatment. His work on the subject appeared in many publications, resulting eventually in his story being brought to the movie screen. But the point is that this prisoner distinguished himself, from a jail cell, through years of study and reading.

(from *Create and Prosper*)

Irving Berlin lost his fortune in the stock market crash of 1929, but he promptly wrote himself into another fortune. He just never stopped trying.

(From a study on creativity)

Noted poet and writer Carl Sandburg once said that all he wanted from life was "enough to eat, time to read, to see some of his work in print occasionally, and to stay out of jail." Who needs a passport or airline ticket? You can walk with the greats through the magic of your library.

(from a study on creativity)

YOU, AS SPEAKER, MUST BE INSPIRED

Napoleon Hill used a special opening in a speech of his called "Mink Coats and Cadillacs." The phrases he uttered did much to let the audience know that he was there as an inspired speaker. Here is what Hill said:

"I've always tried to make each speech better than the last one before. Tonight is no exception. This will be the greatest lecture I've ever given in my life."

Now here are some proven directions for revealing to an audience that you are an inspired speaker:

1. Speak from the heart. This kind of communication is powerful and can inspire.
2. Believe in your material (the subject and material of your speech) so much that it will come across to your audience. Get excited about what you're communicating.
3. Strive to build your speech to a high point of maximum interest. If you can do this, you'll be more likely to keep the maximum attention of your audience.
4. Try to stir your listeners to the very core of their beings. In others words, move them in such a way (by your speech) that they will be different people from that point on.
5. Use the power of your personality to make your material inspiring. A speaker's compelling personality can wring a lot of inspiration out of the spoken word. Make them remember *you* in the weeks and months to come, not just the ABC's of your speech material. Do your best to make them think of you for some time to come as a truly dynamic speaker.

ILLUSTRATIONS AND ANECDOTES CAN BUILD INSPIRATION

Granted that you will speak to an audience more effectively if inspired, you should begin now to collect and save any inspirational illustrations or anecdotes for future speeches.

Illustrations in a speech help a great deal to clarify what is being said and make it more interesting. Illustrations may do any of the following:

- An illustration may offer a comparison.
- An illustration may help to explain an idea, view, belief, or whatever.
- An illustration may describe something so vividly that a listener is moved by it and thus inspired.

In a speech I've given a number of times for various audiences, I wanted the audience to realize how easy today's modern era is compared with the colonial period. I decided to contrast the two time periods with an illustration. Here's an excerpt from the illustration I used:

"An old Italian proverb says that 'he conquers who endures.' The early colonists were victorious over their obstacles because they wouldn't give up. Crossing the ocean in small inadequate boats was no little feat in itself. Many wondered if they would even get to the new land alive. And when they did, the struggle for survival really began. Indian threat, famine, malaria, unfit drinking water, swamps, and having to hunt for food were only a few of their problems. The need to build a fort for protection from the Indians was imperative. To top it all, ships bringing much needed supplies from England got lost or seldom got through. Despite the overwhelming difficulties, a scant hundred years later, colonists in Williamsburg, Virginia, had come amazingly far."

As defined in the *American College Dictionary*, an anecdote is "a narrative of a particular incident or occurrence of an interesting nature." Here's an example:

"While a semi-invalid, Robert Louis Stevenson completed thirty-thousand words of *Dr. Jekyll and Mister Hyde.* When his wife criticized it, after he read it to her, Stevenson became enraged and threw the manuscript into the fire, saying she was right about it. He promptly returned to his bed with pencil and fresh paper. He wrote three more days with little sleep and emerged with a completely new manuscript of the same idea. The slender 149-page book, *The Strange Case of Dr. Jekyll and Mister Hyde,* was published in 1886 for one shilling. When the *London Times* praised the new book, it quickly became a best seller, selling forty-thousand copies in six months."

Keep the following facts about anecdotes in mind:

1. An anecdote is a little story with a point. It usually has a beginning, middle, and end.
2. Your account to an audience of your first day on a new job, the experience of getting married, entering military service, or any number of other experiences could be expressed in anecdote form.
3. A great many people think of anecdotes as short human interest items about practically anything.
4. Your own past experiences, training, education, travels, jobs, and adventures offer a rich seedground for many fine anecdotes. So be sure to research your own memory well, when you're planning a speech to inspire. Try to focus or zero in on inspiring anecdotes from your past.
5. Watch all kinds of publications for possible anecdotes you can use.
6. Friends, relatives, and family members are often a good source of anecdotes.

Many good speakers set up and maintain a series of file cards on all manner of illustrations and anedotes for use in speeches. I urge you to do this too, for it can be of immense help to you when planning future speeches. I suggest that you have at least four headings for your anecdotes:

- Illustrations and anecdotes that inform
- Illustrations and anecdotes that inspire
- Illustrations and anecdotes that persuade
- Illustrations and anecdotes that entertain

The next time you're planning a speech to inform, persuade, inspire, or entertain, you have only to turn to your file cards under the speech purpose of your choice. You'll have a good supply of appropriate anecdotes ready and waiting to use in your speech.

Type or write your anecdotes and illustrations on cards, and keep collecting suitable ones over a period of time. Eventually, you'll accumulate a nice supply for each kind of major speech. I know this system works. I've used it myself for years, and many other speakers do the same.

A double benefit of this file card method is that the same anecdotes can be used in a variety of new speeches. The beauty of this idea is that it enables you to put your hands on just the right illustration or anecdote you need at a given time. That can be very important for an active speaker.

HOW TO TELL IF YOU'RE SUCCEEDING

There are definite ways you can tell if your speech to inspire is really going over well or not. Here are some signs to watch for which reveal whether or not you seem to be accomplishing your purpose:

- The audience before you is sitting there as if spellbound. Most of your listeners appear to be following what you're saying very closely.

- Some individual listeners in the audience may be visibly moved. Some speeches are planned and presented so well that they really get through to listeners and truly inspire them.
- Several or more in the audience are not paying attention, whispering to their neighbors, looking around the room, or obviously have just tuned out.

SOME IDEAS FOR A SPEECH TO INSPIRE

Here are some suggestions for a speech to inspire. I'm sure you'll be able to think of many ideas for this type of speech yourself:

1. "Nothing Can Defeat Man's Indomitable Spirit" (a good idea for a speech encouraging listeners to hang in there and stick to something).
2. "Life Is Still Incredibly Good" (for a speech reminding listeners that despite all the problems of modern day living, life is still good . . . and a wondrous gift).
3. "You Were Born to Be a Champion" (for a speech to inspire listeners to go for the roses, be more successful, and achieve more in life).
4. "Gratitude Adds to your Power" (for a speech meant to inspire listeners to be more grateful for their health, loved ones, and other blessings).
5. "If You Can Read, You're Rich" (for a speech to inspire listeners to appreciate the rewards of reading and to actually read more).

REVIEW POINTS FOR POWERFUL SPEAKING

- The speech to inspire can influence one or more listeners to make their lives count more.

- If you, as the speaker, are inspired, your speech will have a far greater chance to achieve its purpose of inspiring.
- When you speak from the heart, you reveal to the audience that you're inspired.
- It can be a worthy goal to try to stir your listeners to the very core of their being.
- The power of your personality can make the material of your speech more inspiring.
- Illustrations and anecdotes can help build inspiration.
- Collecting illustrations and anecdotes on file cards can pay off later when you need just the right material for one or more speeches.

8

The Speech To Entertain

As you might expect, the purpose of entertaining an audience is an important part of public speaking. Many consider this type of speech to be the most popular, and it may well be their favorite speech to listen to. The spoken word can be a wonderful way to brighten up the lives of audiences. To entertain, then, is to bring pleasure to others. It's a worthy goal.

Another way of defining or thinking of this type of speech is to view it as an after dinner speech. It has long been traditional to expect an after dinner speaker to be an entertaining one, though this doesn't always turn out to be the case. When many groups of people gather to have dinner and then listen to a chosen speaker, people want the speaker to entertain them. Such speeches may also be informative in places, and even include elements of inspiration and persuasion, but the overall purpose is to entertain the audience.

A lot of dinner programs take the time to introduce guests of honor and others at the banquet table and attend to various business mattters of the group or organization, before the main speaker is introduced. Other programs go right to the speaker, as soon as dinner is over. By its very nature, the after dinner speech implies something light and entertaining.

Pick an entertaining subject. You certainly want to avoid any and all dull, lifeless, boring, or uninteresting subjects for this kind of speech. Focus on a subject with the following characteristics:

- Something attractive
- Something amusing
- Something light and sparkling
- Something with a strong degree of interest
- Something with entertainment appeal for the audience

Almost every audience has bored people in it. Who knows what kind of day they may have had? Some of them may be facing all manner of problems, or perhaps already be in the midst of them. There they are, sitting out there looking at you and waiting to hear your speech. Some of them may be secretly daring you to entertain them. Your job is to do just that: entertain them as best you can, to make them feel amused, perhaps to laugh a little, and to go back to their homes and lives feeling lighter, a bit happier, and generally better for the experience.

In a real sense, subjects which offer escape often work well. Through your choice of subject and presentation, it's entirely possible to take your listeners on a journey. Speakers who present programs on travel to exotic lands or glamorous cities are a good example of this escapism benefit. Their programs entertain audiences, while informing them at the same time.

Showmanship helps in this speech. Speakers with a flair or gift for showmanship can put this ability to good use in the speech to entertain. Showmanship is not deceit or trickery; it means to brighten up something and make it attractive, enjoyable, and appealing. True showmanship can be developed over a period of time. Many figures in the entertainment world have this ability. Bob Hope certainly has it. So do Carol Burnett, Johnny Carson, Don Rickles, and a number of others. Watch for other speakers who seem to have this quality, and try to pick up some of their techniques.

HUMOR AND THE SPEECH TO ENTERTAIN

I don't want you to get the idea that the speech to entertain must be completely filled with jokes, witty lines, and cracker-barrel humor. You need not be a funny person in order to entertain an audience. It isn't necessary to saturate your speech with jokes. A great many speeches entertain without relying on a series of jokes.

On the other hand, some humor will add strength to your speech. The thing to shoot for is an overall amusing effect. If your speech succeeds in amusing your audience, you have accomplished the right purpose. Just remember that to be amused, listeners don't have to laugh all the way through your speech. There may be only a few places in your speech which bring a laugh, but if the total effect of your material—meaning your speech as a whole—is amusing, then you have entertained your audience.

One standard definition of humor is "a comic quality causing amusement . . . the humor of a situation." Another definition states that humor "is the faculty of perceiving what is amusing or comical."

In thinking about humor for this type of speech, keep in mind that humor consists of many things:

1. Humor is the fine art of exaggeration.
2. Humor is satire, a play on words, sarcasm.
3. Humor is the ability to take the familiar and make it seem funny.
4. Humor is also association (often unexpected), understatement, and just plain surprise.
5. Humor is irony (saying a thing in such a way that the opposite is obviously intended).

The immortal Will Rogers knew how to use humor, always in good taste, never degrading or cheap. He had a marvelous ability to interpret the events of the day in such a way that it brought pleasure and entertainment to millions of people. Once, Rogers commented: "All senators travel a lot. They all try and keep away from home as much as they can." He also observed: "As our government deteriorates our humor increases."

TIPS ON DEVELOPING AND PRESENTING THE SPEECH TO ENTERTAIN

Here are some proven ways for creating an amusing effect in this kind of speech. Actually, you have a number of options:

- Open your speech with an unusual remark.
- Poke fun at some person in the audience or even yourself.
- Relate an amusing story or anecdote.
- Refer to a humorous experience you've recently had.
- Strive to conclude your speech on an amusing point. Skip any detailed summation for this speech. Use something, preferably funny, which condenses your main points in a nutshell.

Generally speaking, this type of speech fares better with a brisk pace. Don't rush through it, of course, but the pace should be more swift than other types of speeches. Strive also for the following:

- Be positive.
- Be optimistic.
- Be cheerful and good-natured.
- Try to sound friendly and like a good-humored person.
- Act like you're enjoying yourself . . . like you're glad to be there speaking to the audience.

You'll need crisp and vivid illustrations and anecdotes for this kind of speech. Some likely sources for useful illustrations include your own recent amusing experiences, other entertaining things that have happened to you, interesting material from the lives of others you know, family adventures, something you hear on television or read in the comic strips. There's a variety of sources for amusing material.

Better still, you could profit a great deal by starting a humor book or file. Put anything you find entertaining in this book or type up the material on index cards. Then you have only to turn to your special book, file, or index cards for a variety of possible amusing illustrations.

Keep in mind that this speech to entertain needs a structure, a framework, just as the previous ones do. This means an effective introduction, middle part, and conclusion. You'll want a strong beginning, because your audience will decide from your opening whether they want to keep listening to you.

Deal with the main points in the body of your speech as simply as possible. In fact, you should choose very clear points, leading up to each one with an attractive anecdote, story, or illustration.

Don't use all your best material in the early part of your speech. Save some of the most amusing bits for the latter part and ending of the speech.

IDEAS FOR A SPEECH TO ENTERTAIN

Here are some suggestions for a speech to entertain. But again, your own life, experience, and background offer you an excellent source for possible subjects:

1. "Everyone Wants to Do Impressions" (for a speech on the fun of being able to sound like film stars and celebrities)
2. "Applause: Waves of Love" (for a speech on the joys and challenges of being a performer)
3. "Their Names Were Magic" (for a speech on some of the

memorable stars — actors, singers, comedians, dancers — of yesteryear)

4. "How to Feel Laughter Tugging at Your Sleeve" (for a speech on the value and importance of laughter in everyone's life)
5. "Wise Man Say Keep Something for a Rainy Day" (for a speech on preparing for the future, which would also inform as well as entertain)

REVIEW POINTS FOR POWERFUL SPEAKING

- The speech to entertain is often thought of as the after dinner speech.
- The speech to entertain, by its very nature, implies something light and interesting.
- Showmanship can help in the presentation of this kind of speech.
- The objective to shoot for in this speech is an overall *amusing* effect.

9

Grab Their Attention and Hold It

When a television star or well-known celebrity walks out to speak to an audience, or perform for them, the attention of the audience is almost automatically guaranteed. Unfortunately, for people who are not well-known, even if they have a good deal of speaking experience behind them, this isn't the case. The attention of listeners must be grabbed and maintained throughout the speech.

It's an admirable goal for every speaker worth his or her salt. There are specific reasons, beyond the obvious, for wanting to gain an audience's attention. They include the following:

- Having gained attention, you can try for a direct and immediate response, which is important in certain kinds of speeches (the speech to entertain, for one).
- A high attention level sets the stage for communication to take place.
- Audiences in general respect a speaker who is able to get and keep their attention. They may well express interst in having a return visit by this kind of capable and effective speaker.
- Success in gaining attention creates confidence. You may become a very active communicator, once you've developed the skill for grabbing attention.

It's one thing, however, to grab an audience's attention at the opening of a speech and something else to keep that attention through the conclusion. Here is where ability and professionalism are called into play.

The next time you find youself part of an audience, look at the faces of people in the crowd around you. Try to determine how many of those near you are really listening with their full attention. The truth is that many people usually tune out a speaker for varying degrees of time, depending on who the speaker is, how well he or she succeeds in hooking and keeping their attention, and how interested they may be in the subject.

It cannot be emphasized enough to say that one of your all-important objectives in making any kind of speech is to get attention and maintain it until you have brought your material to a satisfying ending.

Once I had a memorable experience at a patriotic Fourth of July program. The scene was a football stadium in Atlanta, Georgia. Soon after the program got underway, with parades and speakers taking part on the stadium grounds below, a fight suddenly broke out in the crowd at the forty-five-yard line. More and more people became involved in the fight, and it was spreading fast. Something had to be done quickly. Police got to the scene quickly, but they couldn't seem to get it under control. There were already too many people fighting.

Then a remarkable thing happened. The band began playing "The Star-Spangled Banner." Almost like magic, everyone stood up. All who had been fighting stopped at once, as if on cue. Our national anthem did in an instant what all the police there that day could not do. I've never forgotten seeing what happened that afternoon. It made a strong impression on me.

I'm not suggesting that *you* perform the national anthem, when and if you should lose the attention of your audience while speaking. But it does show that there are ways to regain attention. And what you need, as aces in the hole, are some methods of your own for leading your audience back to your speech. Better still, try not to lose your listeners in the first place. But if you do, it's nice to have some options in mind for regaining their attention. And that means knowing what to do.

SOME WAYS TO REGAIN ATTENTION

Here are a number of proven ways to recapture the attention of your audience:

1. Try a fairly long pause. This abrupt silence may well rivet their attention on you and your speech again.
2. If you happen to be on a strong point in your speech, pound your fist or hand on the podium. Many may disagree or find fault with this method, but I've seen it work on a number of occasions when observing speakers who have temporarily lost their audiences.
3. Move out to the side of the podium or take a few steps away from where you've been standing. Some speakers never move a foot throughout an entire speech. I've seen even nationally acclaimed speakers move to the front and side of the podium or lectern for the sake of variety. It can help to gain fresh attention.
4. Say something extra startling or dramatic. If your audience has tuned out, you'll have to repeat it a few times, perhaps, before they take it in and respond with new attention.
5. Use a sweeping or dramatic gesture. This is a visual tool worth trying. It works best for speakers who don't use many gestures when speaking. Seeing a sudden wide gesture (made by your arms or hands) will be like a flag-raising in the eyes of your audience, and it may thus call their immediate attention back to your speech.
6. If you've reached a point in your speech close enough to a question-and-answer period (assuming you have planned

one), you could resort to this option and open up your program to questions from the audience. This gets a high new level of attention fast. There are listeners in almost every audience who welcome the opportunity to ask various questions. But to turn suddenly to a question-and-answer session may mean that you'll have to skip important material in your speech. Then, too, you may not wish to include a question-and-answer phase of your program or you may not have time to do so.

7. Resort to a visual aid of some kind. If your speech makes use of posters, charts, signs, drawings, film, slides, or any visual-aids at all, you can try using one to win back your audience. It's the old cliché that *one* picture is worth a thousand words. It may well prove the case in your speech.

If you're going to do well at gaining an audience's attention quickly, you will have to be sure to plan your opening carefully. Ask yourself the following questions:

- What is the *first* thing I can open with in my speech that will hook their attention?
- Is there some type of dramatic or surprise beginning I could use?
- Would a key question or series of questions get their attention?
- How can I make my introduction for this speech different, and especially appealing? For help with this, study and listen carefully to the openings used by other speakers. Take note of the strong openings, the dynamic attention-getters, and why they were successful. Perhaps you can use something similar in your own speech introduction.

The answers to such questions will provide you with a number of choices for the opening of your speech. It is absolutely imperative that you have an attention-getting beginning. Otherwise, your audience may tune out fast, which means that the rest of your speech, however good it may be, will not get across.

DON'T LOSE EYE CONTACT WITH YOUR AUDIENCE

An immediate way to make every speech you give more successful is to make up your mind *now* to know your material so well, on each speaking date, that you won't have to lose eye contact with your audience. Maintaining good eye contact lets your audience know the following:

- You've done your homework. You're not glued to your notes, because you know the material you're presenting.
- You thought enough of the audience and the occasion to be well prepared. In other words, your overall preparation and presentation reveal that you want your speech to be worthwhile for your audience.
- You are dedicated and committed to communicating the material to your listeners.

It can be most distracting when you're forced to continually look at notes, an outline, or full speech manuscript. You are much more likely to achieve a high quality and level of communication if you keep your eyes on the audience for most of your speech (and preferably for all of it).

There are speakers who are so determined not to lose or short-circuit eye contact with their audiences that they refuse to look away from their listeners even on occasions when their minds go completely blank. This can happen to a rather new speaker, and even to a skilled veteran. But you can definitely learn how to handle such temporary mind blanks. What you do is simply think on your feet. Have such a clear idea of what you want to say that, if necessary, you can put it into other words.

HOW TO BE READY FOR THE UNEXPECTED

After you've been speaking before audiences for a few years, you'll realize the truth that there's always the possibility of the unexpected. You, as speaker, have little or no control over planes flying overhead, or police cars, ambulances, or fire engines speeding by with sirens at full blast. You must therefore be ready to cope with such things.

I remember hearing the true story about a guest speaker in a rural church. It was mid-summer and quite hot, as the small church did not have air-conditioning. The person speaking had only a small amount of experience behind him. In the middle of his presentation, his glasses became so cloudy and fogged with the sultry air that he took them off and placed them on the podium for a few minutes. He then went on with his speech. A few moments later, while making a sweeping gesture, he accidentally hit the glasses, sending them flying across the entire front of the church sanctuary.

As you might expect, the congregation of the small church was flabbergasted. But the speaker stayed in control of the situation. Without a word, he simply left the podium, walked down front, and then over to the far side. He leaned down and picked up his glasses, returning then to the podium. "This is the first pair of airborne glasses I've owned. I'll try to keep them grounded for awhile."

This speaker didn't ignore what had happened. He met it head on with a humorous and appropriate remark, and then went right ahead with his speech, which was well received.

The point is that you must be ready to handle the unexpected. You might speak for six months at various places, without one mishap taking place, and then find yourself in a cycle of surprising events connected with your speaking. The important thing is how you react to them. Don't let it throw you and ruin the program you have planned for the audience. Instead, as the old saying goes, "go on with the show." Your audience will respect you for it.

REVIEW POINTS FOR POWERFUL SPEAKING

- Grab the audience's attention fast, and try to hold it throughout your speech.
- Remember that some persons in every audience may tune out for a varying degree of time.
- Use a long pause occasionally. It's one way to regain attention.
- Seek ways to make your speech both appealing and interesting to an audience.
- Maintain good eye contact with your audience. It's a sign that you've done some good advance preparation.
- Be ready and able to cope with unexpected events which may take place when you're speaking.

10

Examples Are the Life of a Speech

This chapter reveals one of the tried and proven secrets of becoming a dynamic and successful speaker. This secret is simply the art of using anecdotes, examples, and stories to illustrate what you're saying. If there's one thing in a speech that helps you to communicate, it's good examples. They not only transmit information and vital points to be remembered by an audience, they often do it with charm and unforgettable vividness.

To a considerable degree, these supporting stories can bring a speech to life and make the audience interested in what comes next. Take a look at the following examples about being persistent and hanging in there:

EXAMPLE: When Winston Churchill found the going rough, as a young journalist trying to sell his material, he didn't waste time having the blues about it. He buckled down and tried three times as hard.

EXAMPLE: Cole Porter, the great musical show writer and composer, was thirty-eight before his success began in a big way. But he had been writing songs since he was a small boy. He had even had some shows on Broadway, but success kept eluding him. He wouldn't give up, though; he just kept on creating songs.

On his way to Europe, aboard ship, Porter met a producer who talked to him about a new musical for Broadway and asked Porter to do the music. After this chance meeting, Porter's career began to soar. But the point is that he stayed in there trying to find his place until age thirty-eight. Just a few of the lucky results for the world are such all-time great numbers as "Night and Day," "I've Got You Under My Skin," "I Love Paris," "In the Still of the Night," and a long list of other Cole Porter standards.

HOW TO BECOME A MASTER AT USING EXAMPLES

Once you have a growing file or collection of ancedotes, stories, and examples, you can begin to develop more skill at making use of them in your speaking. Here are some directions for achieving this goal:

1. File or group your illustrations under various subject categories such as love, friendship, military, patriotism, general interest, achieving success, financial, ESP, and on down the line.
2. Save good examples you find about various vocations and professions, such as farmers, lawyers, doctors, nurses, teachers, dentists, and musicians. Over a period of time you can build a worthy collection of very useful stories. Then, whenever you need one or more illustrations about certain job fields, you'll have your own handy file.
3. Take an old speech of yours and try to pick suitable examples for it from your special file. This will increase your ability to select the right stories to illustrate your speeches.
4. Even if you don't have a speech to plan and present in the near future, choose a subject to your liking and try your hand at developing the idea. As your speech grows, look over your example file carefully and choose the most effective stories for the speech.

5. Save and collect effective anecdotes about the lives and careers of famous people, including film stars and celebrities. They will add interest to a speech, because most audiences (and people in general) enjoy hearing about famous people.

You can, of course, also learn more about the art of using effective examples by listening carefully to a variety of good speakers and taking notes on the illustrations they use. This is not stealing; you may be able to put an example you hear, and decide to use, into your own words.

Wherever you live, chances are excellent that both unknown and famous speakers will be in your area to present speeches or programs. I urge you to go to hear them. You can learn a lot by listening to them and discovering how they weave illustrations throughout their speeches.

A new trend is evident regarding today's visiting speakers. A number of well-known speakers (especially specialists in certain subjects like sales, success motivation, real estate, and advertising) are banding together increasingly to offer all-day speech seminars for the public. For a fee of $15 to $25 (or more in some cases at this writing), listeners hear one speech after another by experts and authorities on specific subjects. The fee usually includes lunch in the day's planned program.

These speakers rent an auditorium for the day, plan a theme around their total program, and advertise the all-day seminar in national or local newspapers and trade magazines. These full day programs are presented in leading cities in the United States, and sometimes overseas as well.

If you prefer not to pay for the privilege of hearing a speaker, you have the option of attending other programs presented in your area. Colleges and universities, for example, frequently present a variety of speakers. There is little or no charge, depending on who the speaker is and the nature of the program.

Ads and notices sometimes appear in daily newspapers, announcing the program topics of a particular individual speaker in town. I once noticed such an announcement in a Memphis newspaper, attended the free program, and learned that the same speaker offered other speeches on a weekly basis. I went to many of the programs. There was no charge at all, other than a free-will contribution to help defray the cost of this local speaker's expenses. I got a lot of useful information by listening to this speaker.

You can often hear speakers, without having to pay, in any number of churches. Many churches offer family night and general fellowship meetings.

THE ILLUSTRATIONS OF BILLY GRAHAM

For a strong example of the art of effective illustration in action, listen to evangelist Billy Graham. He's a master at using examples via the spoken word. Whether you hear him in person or on television (he also has a radio program), you'll discover the following truths about his use of illustrations:

1. Graham's examples are powerful. They frequently stir his listeners.
2. His anecdotes and stories are often used to support certain points, clarify them and help to persuade or convince listeners.
3. Billy Graham knows how to select and use unforgettable examples. They stick in one's memory, long after his message and program have ended.

There's no doubt that Billy Graham would have been one of the most successful sales executives in the world, had he chosen that route instead of the religious one. He is certainly one of the best and most dynamic speakers of the century. He communicates. Thousands of people who have heard him at one time or another have commented on his remarkable speaking ability, whether they went along with his religious persuasions or not.

THE RIGHT AND WRONG KINDS OF EXAMPLES

As you plan the material for your speeches, stay aware that there are right and wrong kinds of examples. The more selective you are in choosing which ones to use, the stronger your speech will be. Here are some useful pointers:

- Choose illustrations that have a direct relation to the point you wish to make or support.
- Avoid using off-color or distasteful stories.
- Watch the length of the illustrations you plan to use. If your speech is a fairly long one, relating an extended anecdote may be unwise (particularly if you're pressed for time). Try to vary the examples you use, presenting both short and some not-too-long ones, as your time allows.
- The more examples you have available, the better able you will be to use the cream-of-the-crop ones. In other words, if you have a wide choice open to you, go with the four-star choice illustrations.
- Don't use vague or confusing illustrations. You want your audience to grasp the point or meaning behind the story at once, and that calls for the use of examples that clearly relate to, explain or support your point.

WHAT THE AUDIENCE MAY REMEMBER ABOUT YOUR SPEECH

Many a speaker would be surprised to know what one or more audiences actually remember about a given speech. As speaker, you can't be sure that you have achieved your desired purpose — even though some of those in your audience may later give indication, by their remarks and reactions, that you in fact did succeed.

Here are a number of random responses to the question of what was remembered about certain speeches. These comments are taken from my notes and files in the basic speech classes I taught at Murray State University, in Kentucky:

"*The speaker was too visibly nervous.*" (Note here that what was remembered was something dealing with the presentation of the speech and not its content.)

"*I remember the part about Harry Truman believing that one must stay in good physical condition and that when the legs go, it isn't long before the rest follows.*"

"*I remember the place in her speech where she forgot what came next. She didn't let this ruin her speech. She handled it well.*" (Again what was remembered was the presentation and not the content.)

"*The techniques of McGuffey in doing their reader books stuck in my mind.*" (content)

"*I was surprised to know there are so many verbal blunders.*"

"*The thing I remember most is the friendliness of the speaker. It made me want to listen more carefully.*"

Use interesting, provocative, or supporting examples throughout your speeches. A special illustration hooks attention well, and thus may work in the beginning. One that summarizes the core of your speech and wraps it all up nicely can be used in a conclusion. Generally speaking, however, most speech illustrations come in the body or middle section of the material, where you need to reinforce the main points with supporting materials.

HOW TO CREATE NEW SPEECH EXAMPLES

It may happen on occasion that you can't find the right example for a certain speech. Should this happen to you, create some new ones. I once planned a speech on the subject of love ("A Great Love Can Change Lives"). When I couldn't find the existing examples I wanted, I created my own. I used some facts of literature to do it, of course, but I put them into my own words:

EXAMPLE: The love of a little girl transformed the life of an old man named Silas Marner, in the immortal book. (I then expanded on this to finish the example.)

EXAMPLE: Poet Robert Browning's love for Elizabeth Barrett changed the face of all the world for her. (I then expanded on this to complete the illustration.)

Remember, when and if you can't find the example you want, consider creating your own by placing it into your own words. The way to do it is to list the facts you need to demonstrate. Then try to relate them in an interesting way. If what you want to say deals with a person, you must stick to what actually did happen, but you can say it in your own words.

Using just a few basic historic facts, here's a fairly short example I created and have used many times to support the point that glory and fame are fleeting: "In the glory days of ancient Rome, victorious warriors returned to the Eternal City in the midst of great fanfare and celebration. Large crowds gathered to cheer them, as they rode into the city on chariots. But legend says that beside them also rode a slave carrying a sign reminding everyone that all glory is fleeting."

REVIEW POINTS FOR POWERFUL SPEAKING

- Good examples help to bring a speech to life and make it more interesting to hear.
- Collect stories, facts and anecdotes under various subject headings. Then when you need one or more examples, you have only to choose from your own handy file.
- Listen to a variety of speakers, to see (among other things)

how they weave examples throughout their speeches.

- A new trend today is all-day seminars by visiting speakers, who are experts and authorities on certain subjects like real estate, ESP, marketing-advertising, stock investment, and others.
- Billy Graham is a speaker who knows how to select and use unforgettable illustration-examples.

11

Gestures Make a Difference

Audiences vary in their appreciation of speakers, and in the reasons they like certain speeches. Many members of an audience may not even be aware of the fact that one speaker uses more and better gestures than another one. But these same people just know, instinctively, that they liked certain speakers better, summing up their feelings with the comment: "He (or she) got the material over to us."

Getting the material over is often difficult. A useful and helpful tool for speaking to an audience is the gesture. It's interesting to imagine what communicating might be like using only gestures. The silent screen stars had to act this way for their movie roles, before the talkies came along.

As a speaker, you have a right to express your personality. If it is natural for you, by all means talk with your hands (that is, use various gestures to let your hands support what you're saying). Gesture is an art. It is an international language. The hand alone uses levels, planes, and positions when communicating. A shrug of the shoulders is still used to mean something is unclear. A nod of the head stands for yes. The open hand (palm showing) stretched out before a speaker still usually means stop.

The gesture is a movement meant to add communication

power to what is being transmitted to listeners. Here are some sound reasons for using them in a speech:

1. A gesture can strengthen a statement.
2. A gesture can help to clarify something.
3. Gestures help a speaker describe something to an audience ("big as a breadbasket," "as long as from where I'm standing to the back of this hall").
4. Certain types of gestures reveal the confidence and conviction of a speaker.
5. A speaker looks too wooden and lifeless, if he or she just stands there the whole time, without using any gestures at all.
6. Gestures can add extra touches of power to a speech.

There are, on the other hand, objections or negative views regarding gestures. Here are some of the most frequently voiced reasons for not using gestures (or at least not many of them):

1. Gestures look phony when used by many speakers.
2. Gestures can be distracting to some people in an audience. This is especially true if the speaker goes overboard and uses far too many gestures.
3. Gestures aren't necessarily proof of sincerity.
4. The audience may focus on the gestures of the speaker (if a lot of them) instead of the material of the speech itself.
5. Too many gestures may be an attempt by the speaker to hide nervousness. (A lot of them may well mean an open sign of nervousness.)
6. Some gestures just don't look natural. They appear to be forced or contrived, even though the speaker tries his or her best.

Judging by the speeches presented by a variety of speakers, the most effective speakers (meaning the best ones) do use some gestures.

Sometimes body movements other than calculated gestures can be highly distracting to an audience. I still remember hearing a preacher in North Carolina who never gestured with his arms or hands. He never moved to the side of the pulpit and rarely, if ever, moved a foot away while speaking. His one very distracting habit was the way he bobbed backward and forward on the heels of his feet. This went on sometimes for almost the entire length of the sermon. I noticed that many listeners in the congregation seemed bored and inattentive to what he was saying. He may not have realized that he bobbed while speaking, but he kept it up continually during the several occasions I heard him speak. Some arm and hand gestures by this man, and a halt of the bobbing, would have helped the communication process a great deal.

SOME SPEAKERS DON'T KNOW WHAT TO DO WITH THEIR HANDS

Always know what to do with your hands when presenting a speech. Many don't. Clasping your hands behind your back looks awkward. One hand in a pocket is definitely not recommended either. The best thing to do with your arms is to keep them naturally at your sides. This way your arms are free to make gestures, to turn over note cards, the pages of a manuscript, and are generally ready for action. For some variety, you can place one hand on the side of the lectern or podium.

In order to turn over the note cards of your speech (if you use them), or the manuscript pages, you'll need one hand and possibly two (especially if you're speaking outside or in a drafty hall).

The following reactions to the gestures of speakers were taken from notes I made when teaching some college speech classes. All these particular speakers were college students:

- "Good use of the yardstick to make gestures and to point out chart material."
- "The speaker at one point had his elbow on the podium."
- "The gestures in this speech called 'Let Hands Talk' were especially effective and covered the full range. This was the best use of gestures I've seen in the class to date."
- "She kept her arms behind her back most of the time. I only saw two gestures, and they looked forced."
- "This speaker needs to make wider gestures. The ones I saw seemed too narrow."

JOHN KENNEDY'S ARTFUL USE OF THE JAB

John Kennedy was an admirable speaker. His posture was always good, his voice clear and strong, and he had the ability to make an audience *believe* what he said.

Kennedy liked to make frequent use of the jab (in the air) with one hand. To do this, he used the diagonal side of his hand. This evidently helped him to emphasize the words of his statements and seemed at times to instill in them a life of their own. The artful one-hand-in-the-air jab almost became his trademark, and a great many people remember him this way, jabbing the air with his hand to add force to his points. Ted Kennedy uses the jab too, and he is also a considerably forceful and skilled speaker, as he proved at the Democratic convention of 1980.

You can practice this jab, yourself, in the mirror. When you believe you've got it to the point where it looks natural, it can prove to be a useful gesture in your future speeches. But don't of course overdo it. Use it along with other gestures as well.

BILLY GRAHAM'S WIDE USE OF GESTURES

For one of the strongest examples of the art of gesturing, I again recommend that you watch and even study Billy Graham when he speaks. As you might expect from such a dynamic communicator, Graham uses a variety of gestures including the following:

1. Both hands in the air
2. One hand gestures for emphasis
3. He moves u to the right of the lectern-pulpit.
4. He moves out to the left of the pulpit.
5. The diagonal jab in the air with one hand.

Graham also uses other gestures such as holding the open Bible in one outstretched hand, which is quite effective. But the above listed gestures are those which you can use in your own speeches.

YOUR OWN USE OF GESTURES

You should definitely plan to use at least *some* gestures in your speeches. They will be better because of them. If you discover that your hands want to do even more, and try to talk for you, try to control the urge to use too many gestures. If your hands are constantly involved in a variety of gestures, it may look forced, overdone and artificial, depending of course on the overall ability and degree of skill you reveal. In general, it's usually better to use fewer gestures which look and are genuine. When gestures aren't overdone, moreover, it also means that the ones you do use Wwill be that much more meaningful and important. In the next chapter, we'll take a look at the use of emotion in public speaking.

REVIEW POINTS FOR POWERFUL SPEAKING

- A speaker has a right to feel free to express his or her personality.

- Gestures can support what you're saying and add emphasis, animation, and life to your speeches.
- Gesture is an art.
- John Kennedy was known for his artful use of the jab (with one hand).
- Billy Graham uses a number of powerful gestures, which add to the total strength of his speaking.
- Strive to use at least some gestures in your speeches, but see that they're natural and not forced or artificial ones.

12

Techniques of Emotional Appeal

Your ability to reach and stir the emotions of listeners can result in true oratory. Aristotle believed that persuasion in every case is effected by appealing to the emotions, by giving the right impression of the speaker's character (meaning your own), or by proving the truth of the statements made.

Think back on the speeches you've heard either live or on radio-television. The truly great speeches affected their listeners' feelings; most of the people who heard them were profoundly moved.

You can reach listeners, persuade them, and move them to action by appealing to emotions such as:

- Love
- Hatred
- Fear
- Freedom
- Confidence
- Friendship
- Pride

THE USE OF EMOTION IN THE MAIN SPEECHES OF DOUGLAS MACARTHUR AND JOHN KENNEDY

MacArthur's speech defending his conduct of the war in Korea was delivered before a joint session of Congress on April 19, 1951. The speech came after President Truman abruptly recalled him from his posts in the Far East. Perhaps the most famous and most often quoted line of this speech came near the end, when MacArthur mentioned how he still remembered the refrain of one of the most popular barracks ballads of that day which proclaimed most proudly that "old soldiers never die; they just fade away."

Reactions to MacArthur's speech were mixed. One sympathetic Congressional hearer said: "We saw a great hunk of God in the flesh, and we heard the voice of God." Much of the criticism and comment seemed to be a blend of happy emotionalism and philosophical commentary. Hubert Humphrey reacted this way:

> General MacArthur's speech was a masterful presentation by a persuasive man rising at a dramatic occasion to give reason and justification for his life's work and life's reputation. There is no doubt that it affected every member of the Congress who heard him. With the fading away of emotions and the supremacy of reason, the American people will come to see that President Truman was correct in removing General MacArthur.

Many felt, as Humphrey did, that the speech was highly charged with emotion. When a great military leader speaks before Congress and fifty million Americans to justify his life's work and reputation, it seems only natural that such a speech would be filled to the brim with emotion.

Gary Cronkhite, in an article for *The Quarterly Journal of Speech,* defines emotion as "activation," or level of arousal. Evaluating emotional appeal consists of estimating the sum of the motivational strengths or the impact of the verbal stimuli used to represent these motivational concepts.

Certainly contributing to the emotional climate of MacArthur's speech were the facts of the drama, glamor, and emotional partisanship that surrounded the event. Many Democrats saw his speech and MacArthur, himself, as a threat to the incumbent administration. Senator Mundt, a former teacher of public address, stated that the speech "seems destined to become one of the classics of the English language."

MacArthur's emotional proof was strong. Aristotle states in his *Rhetoric* that the speaker's language will be "appropriate if it expresses emotion and character and does not speak casually about weighty matters, nor solemnly about trivial ones." MacArthur certainly did not speak casually. Most of the critics previously cited agreed that he spoke eloquently. A study of the speech reveals his strong character, through the use of language.

The emotions of love and friendship are quite evident in the speech. Perhaps this can best be seen in a comment the General made shortly before he gave his speech, when he was asked about his politics. He replied: "The only politics I have is contained in a single phrase known well to all of you— 'God Bless America.' " His great love for his country is a dominant emotion that can hardly be missed in the speech. He showed the audience he had love, that he was just, and he did so through his handling of the speech materials.

Another evident emotion in the speech is hatred; his hatred for war and the anguish it causes. The emotion of fear is strong and is clear in his remarks about communism not being stopped in its global conquest, unless it be stopped in both Europe and Asia. The emotion of confidence was revealed in his tribute to the American fighting men; their bravery and their spirit. His admiration for those under his command is a key emotion. All this emotional proof did much, along with his other appeals, to lead his listeners to a single destination of persuasion.

Eugene Knepprath and Theodore Clevenger, in an article

entitled. "Reasoned Discourse and Motive Appeals in Selected Political Speeches," stated that "the words or ideas of a speech are persuasive when they stir up appropriate feelings in the listeners. To that end the speaker tries to select ideas which are concerned with subjects that matter to the listener. We suggest that emotional proofs are concerned with the content of a unit of discourse."

MacArthur's choice of words and ideas did stir up his listeners. Proof of it is the fact that after his speech, many Americans wanted him to run for the Presidency. The very opening of his speech revealed the humanity and pride, the friendliness, sincerity, knowledge of his subject, and his tremendous love of country. After all he had already done, he still wished to serve. Such devotion is bound to stir listeners: "I address you with neither rancor nor bitterness in the fading twilight of life, with but one purpose in mind: to serve my country."

One of the key lines in his speech was: "In war there is no substitute for victory." The speaker made it clear that he was for ending the Korean conflict as soon as possible, had a plan to do so, but was prevented from executing it. The implication was that our government leaders did not want victory. The anguish and anxiety caused him by the bloodshed of the war was bound to have been felt by millions of listeners. But at the close, when the General flashbacked to his oath on the plain at West Point and the "old soldiers never die" quote, he was at the highest point of emotion.

THE KENNEDY SPEECH

There was emotion, too, in John Kennedy's inaugural address, and a comparison of the two speeches is worth noting. Kennedy's inaugural address was essentially a plea to unite, but it was at the same time a vivid description of what he called the new frontier. "Together let us explore the stars, conquer the deserts, eradicate disease, tap the ocean depths and encourage the arts and commerce."

He tied his basic appeals to feelings of security and happiness, not pure emotions, but rather wants and desires. The key image he chose to project was a new frontier.

Aristotle would have liked the speech, for Kennedy was a student of human nature. He and MacArthur both skillfully used metaphor in their speeches. Lines from his speech like "the jungle of suspicion" prove it.

The dominant idea of loyalty was used artfully, and Kennedy backed what he said with example: "Since this country was founded, each generation of Americans has been summoned to give testimony to its national loyalty. The graves of young Americans who answered the call to service surround the globe."

Kennedy appealed to America's sense of duty and responsibility, but his constant goal was a *united* people in performing this duty:

> Now the trumpet summons us again — not as a call to bear arms, though arms we need; not as a call to battle, though embattled we are; but a call to bear the burden of a long twilight struggle, year in and year out, rejoicing in hope, patient in tribulation; a struggle against the common enemies of man: tyranny, poverty, disease and war itself.

Kennedy used short sentences in his speeches, descriptive phrases, and believable supporting materials for his main points. He had an unusual voice with good variety and contrast. His keen sense of history comes across in many of his speeches. In his inaugural, he spoke of defending freedom in its "hour of maximum danger." He said he welcomed this responsibility to defend liberty, and he shared his view that no Americans would exchange places with other peoples or other generations. This was a great tribute to the American people, as well as a challenge: "The energy, the faith, the devotion which we bring to this endeavor (the defense of freedom) will light our country and all who serve it."

A good example of Kennedy's skillful use of language can be seen in his statement about negotiation: "Let us never negotiate out of fear, but let us never fear to negotiate." Above all, he communicated his own desire not only for peace, but for a better, united, and happier world.

A COMPARISON OF THE SPEECHES

In comparing the two speakers (MacArthur and Kennedy), it's wise to keep in mind a vivid statement by Aristotle to the effect that one who appeals to human emotions always makes his audience *feel* with him, even when there is nothing in his arguments. In the case of MacArthur and Kennedy, there was plenty in each argument: the quicker ending of the war by the attainment of victory (in MacArthur's speech) and the premise of Kennedy that a *united* and determined people can indeed achieve and maintain a new frontier of life and happiness.

Both speakers had effective style and both had dramatic delivery, MacArthur with his penetrating voice and Kennedy with his stylish confidence. Both made their audiences well-disposed toward them in the early parts of their speeches. They hooked the attention of their audiences quickly and kept it and chose not only the right words for the occasions, but very forceful words. There are very few long and involved sentences in either speech. (What long sentences there are, are usually broken into simple phrases).

Also, in both cases, there was unity of expression. Both speakers appealed to the senses of duty, pride, friendship, adventure, and exultation. They fulfilled Aristotle's concept that after the facts are presented, the one doing the speaking must excite the listener's emotions.

A close study of both speeches reveals that the dominant appeal in each address was that of love of country and pride in it. Both speakers made the audience *feel* the emotion within them. MacArthur made his audience feel what was in his own heart, as he stood on the rostrum defending his actions. In so doing, he stirred his listeners in a powerful way ("an old soldier who tried to do his duty as God gave him the light to see that duty"). He was a proud, dramatic, powerful personality suddenly recalled from his high post. Much of his speech reviewed his military career. But it also dealt with world strategy, not just the limited war in Korea.

One reason for the success of Kennedy's speech was the sense of identification which came across in it. Everyone wants to end war, to do away with disease, advance as a people and as a nation, make more money, and the rest. The speech leads one to think that Kennedy was trying to speak to *all* Americans, not just to certain segments of society.

Kennedy's appeal for union brought to mind the inaugural address of Thomas Jefferson in 1801. Kennedy's knowledge and love of history were quite evident in his speech. There was strong emotion that day all around him. The way he handled his speech materials, like MacArthur, revealed character.

This is not to say that you have to be a world-famous figure or personality in order to present a memorable speech. What I do wish to suggest is that your ability to appeal to the *basic human emotions* can and will improve the speeches you give. Every time you plan a new speech, think about the appeals you might use to arouse the emotions. Many speeches won't accomplish this, perhaps due to the nature of the subject. But it's quite true that a great many people are reached and stirred via their emotions. If you're trying to persuade an audience, for example, you may come much closer to achieving your purpose with emotional appeals in your speech. You need not seek to arouse emotions in every speech you present. But on some occasions, when you're speaking on a subject very close to you, or one that calls for some action by the audience, it's at least helpful to know about emotional appeals. There is no doubt that many of the memorable and influential speeches have included various emotional appeals. This is one way to reach audiences, but it's your decision as to whether to use such appeals.

REVIEW POINTS FOR POWERFUL SPEAKING

- The ability to stir the emotions of listeners can result in true oratory.
- Some have criticized Billy Graham for emotional approaches, but the evangelist has obtained good results.
- The strongest appeal evident in the speeches of Douglas MacArthur and John Kennedy (their best known addresses) was that of love of country.

13

The Four Ways to Present Your Speech

A major decision regarding the one or many speeches you may present in the future is that of presentation. How should you deliver your speech? This chapter will be of help to you, whenever you must decide which way to present your speech. There are four key ways to give a speech. Some would say five. By trying each of the major methods of delivery, you can discover which type of presentation you prefer to use.

The four ways to give a speech include knowing the speech so well that you need nothing to remind yourself what to say; the use of notes; using only an outline; and speaking from memory. There's another method, which is the use of a full manuscript, but this isn't really an effective form of presentation. If you have your whole speech written down in front of you, you will probably tend to read it, and lose valuable eye contact with your audience. You may have tried a few or all four of these speaking methods. If not, experiment with each one and see what you think.

Let's take a look at the four methods and see how the advantages of each can be applied in your own speaking. First, why is it that not using any tools at all is a good way to speak? It's one of the best, because you are in *constant contact* with your audience. In other words, probably the best way of all to present a speech is to know it so well that you simply stand up on your two feet, look them in the eye, and present your speech.

But how many speakers really feel confident enough to speak this way? Many get the jitters just thinking about it. This method, however, is the four-star way to speak, in the opinion of many. Your decision to choose this way of presentation should depend on how much preparation time you can devote to the speech and the length of your speech. This means going over your speech so many times that you feel you know it very well indeed. Don't memorize the speech; just know it so well—the ideas you wish to communicate—that you're convinced you can present it most exfectively.

There are actually two ways you can present a speech in this knowing-it-so-well manner. First, just speak without any notes at all. You'll know when you're ready to speak this way, by having gone over your speech so often that you feel highly confident and ready. Master the key sections and points of your speech to such an extent that there's virtually no way you can mess up. Even if you do fail to say something in the way in which you practiced it, you can express the same thought in different words. A second way to present your speech in this knowing-it-so-well manner is with index cards.

SPEAKING WITH AN OUTLINE

A second popular way to speak is with an outline. Some outlines are elaborate plans with numerous headings and sub-headings; others are basically simple. If you like the idea of using an outline, decide to write a detailed outline or a more simple one.

You may want a more involved outline if the speech is a long and fairly technical one. If you decide on a simple form of outline, you might just list the essential points you wish to get across in the introduction, middle part, and conclusion of your speech. Use the large letter, number, and small letter outline system, or just list what you intend to do in the three major sections of your speech. Perhaps you have a dramatic story to tell, as an introduction to your speech. If so, indicate that story on your outline under "introduction."

EXAMPLE: Introduction — Story on the increasing number of people who are combining vacations with business trips.

EXAMPLE: Simple outline:
Introduction — Cite the need for additional sources of income today.
Middle part — Give main points and supporting materials for each.
Conclusion — Close with summary or effective anecdote-illustration.

EXAMPLE: Large letter, number, and small letter outline

A. Introduce speech by giving some of the most shocking crime figures.
B. First main point — Today's society is a violent one.
    1. Illustration of brutal murder of nurse in St. Louis.
        a. Cite testimony of experts.
        b. Give reasons for the crime.

Keep in mind the traditional framework of every speech. There's an old saying that describes what a speaker seeks to do in every speech. First, tell them what you're going to say (introduction). Then actually tell them (the body or middle of your speech). And finally, tell them what you've already told them (the conclusion). This sounds overly simplified, but it's worth remembering. Audiences in general do like attention-getting introductions, clear transitions into the body of the speech, and an effective summary or conclusion which wraps it all up neatly.

One advantage of speaking from an outline is that you can often get all of it on a single page or two. Though it depends upon where you're speaking, of course, it can sometimes present problems to have to arrange a stack of three-by-five-inch index cards (or larger ones) before you begin to speak. They can slip out of your hands or off the podium. They can also get into the wrong order. A one or two page outline may be easier to manage than a bunch of cards. It depends on one's individual preference. You should really try both methods for yourself.

I urge you to type or print clearly, whether you use the card system or an outline. Use large, easy-to-read letters. Double-space your outline and use only *one* side of the paper. This helps to insure that you won't lose your place and that your eye can quickly follow the notes, outline, or material written on index cards.

SPEAKING FROM NOTES

Presenting a speech with the use of notes is a third possibility. The notes that speakers use range from key phrases to complete ideas to be communicated. The notes are just *reminders* you have in front of you, to glance at now and then during your speech. Many speakers use some type of notes even for short speeches.

Your speaking notes might simply be a list of directions to yourself. For example: "Give the Winston Churchill quote," or "describe a Hawaiian sunset," or "summarize the speech by repeating the main points."

If you like the idea of using notes when speaking, experiment to find what form of notes works best for you — a number of key words, a basic list of directions, or more extensive notes. Again, the notes you use may range from very simple ones to elaborate pages of many details.

SPEAKING FROM MEMORY

A fourth way of handling a speech is to memorize it. You take nothing at all with you to the speaking platform; you depend completely on your ability to remember your speech material. It goes without saying that if you choose this method, you've got to be very sure that your memory won't fail you.

Some speakers who have used this memory method claim that it has some real advantages. For one thing, you never lose eye contact with your audience. You don't have to bother with notes, an outline, or anything else. You get up on your feet, look at members of your audience in the eye, and give your speech. There are speakers who do seem to be quite effective in this manner. But bear in mind that until you gain experience and skill at speaking from memory alone, there's always the gnawing chance that your mind will suddenly *blank out* at any point in your speech.

It does take a moment to try to remember the next part of the speech. If you can't, stop trying. Instead, try to say what was intended in your own words.

Another consideration about speaking from memory is that audiences are sometimes irritated by speakers who sound like they're delivering a canned, parrot-like routine. If presented in a sing-songy way, without enough pauses, voice variety, and emphasis in the right places, it may sound as if you're speaking by rote. The audience will know for sure that the speech was memorized. And they may wish it hadn't been.

Keep in mind also that it usually takes a good deal of time to memorize most speeches, unless they're fairly short ones. If you try the memory method, you will find a tape-recorder quite helpful. You can then hear for yourself if your speech has too much of that memorized sound to it. By practicing it aloud, to get it down strongly in your memory, you can also work at improving your voice quality, variety, and gestures.

TRY ALL FOUR METHODS

To find which of the four methods of presentation will work most effectively for you, experiment with all of them. Remember, the extemporaneous method, in which you use no notes or only very simple phrases, can be quite effective. If you decide not to use this method, however, choose one of the others. You will need some kind of solid, written framework for your speech, whether you use it in the presentation or not.

David Berlo's summary of the purpose of communication is well worth remembering: "There's real purpose in communicating: the words we can command, and the way we put them together affect what we think about, how we think, and whether we are thinking at all."

It does make good sense to experiment with all of the main ways to present a speech, until you believe you've found the best method for you. If you have a good memory and the time to memorize, this choice might work well for you. An outline or notes, on the other hand, give you some insurance when and if you should run into trouble when presenting your speech. What works well for one speaker may not of course be the best choice for another one. In the next chapter, we'll look at what I believe would be the very best way to deliver your speeches.

REVIEW POINTS FOR POWERFUL SPEAKING

- There are four key ways to present a spe.ch.
- An outline used to present a speech may be an elaborate one or basically simple.
- Many speakers prefer to use some form of notes for their speeches.
- Depending upon your memory alone, in presenting a speech, can be risky.
- It's a good idea to experiment with the various methods of presenting your speech, in order to find which one works best for you.

14

An Ideal Method of Speaking

This chapter reveals more information on what I firmly believe is the ideal way in which to present a speech. As we learned in the last chapter, you can speak from memory, use a full manuscript, an outline, or speak from notes alone. I've tried all these options and am here to tell you that they don't measure up to the power of the extemporaneous method.

By the extemporaneous method, I don't mean that you stand up and speak without any previous preparation. That form of communication is usually referred to as *impromptu* speaking.

The extemporaneous method consists of plenty of advance preparation regarding the material of your speech. You know very clearly what you want to say, but you leave the exact way in which you will communicate it open until the time of presentation.

RECOMMENDED STEPS OF THE IDEAL METHOD

Here are the steps of this ideal way to present a speech. By using them, as a guide, and perfecting the extemporaneous method, you'll have the knowledge of what I'm convinced is the best way to communicate with an audience:

1. Decide on the purpose and subject of your speech. Set a title for it and think about what the material will consist of.
2. Plan the introduction and conclusion of your speech.
3. Select what main points you will use and the supporting materials for each one of them.
4. Find key examples, anecdotes, quotations, and statistics (if any) to illustrate your speech.

PRESENTING YOUR SPEECH

When you've planned the material and structure of your speech, here are the directions I recommend for presenting it to an audience:

1. Before the day or evening of your speech, type or write out on index cards the key lead line or phrase of each section of your speech. All you need write on each card (at the top) is a cue line or phrase. Then number the cards, to help keep them in proper order. The idea of this card system is simple. The one line or phrase on each card will serve as a beacon to remind you what comes next in your speech.
2. Learn the material of your speech exceptionally well. You can do this by going over it many times. The idea is to set up a pattern in your mind. Know what each section of your speech consists of and what thoughts or ideas are being communicated.

   I don't at all mean to suggest by this that you memorize the material (unless you want to). Just know what it essentially says. Know what it is you want to convey to your audience. Simply reading over the plan and material of your speech many times will get you very familiar with it. Study it so well that you feel confident about its presentation.
3. If you wish, let a friend or family member be your audience, while you present the speech for practice. You don't have to give the speech the same way you will when you're

actually before a full audience, and you probably won't. The idea of the extemporaneous method is that you know the speech content very well indeed . . . so well that the presentation of it takes care of itself. So you don't focus on exactly how you will communicate it. You trust yourself to deliver it effectively when the time comes.

4. On the day or night of your speech, place your index cards on the lectern in the order of your speech plan. Make sure the cards are secure and that nothing will get them out of place or knock them on the floor.

Having done all the above, you're now ready to begin your speech. And here you will see the beauty and benefits of this method. You are introduced as the speaker. You rise and walk to the podium or lectern. The big moment has arrived.

You glance down at your neat stack of cards. The first card has only one phrase on it, which is all you need to see. For example, let's say that you're speaking on the subject of creativity. The phrase on your first card reads: "Introduce speech with Canadian pianist illustration." Remember now, you've already done your preparation. Reading the phrase triggers your mind, and you go right into the introduction.

After the introduction you turn to the phrase or line at the top of the next card. It reads: "Give examples of how listener can become more creative." Again, that's all you need to know. You proceed with a series of examples telling how each listener in your audience has the potential power to increase his or her creative ability.

And so it goes. The line or phrase on each card triggers your mind, and you move forward in your speech. Now you may not even need to look at the cards you have placed on the podium. You may know the thought and idea content of your speech so well that it's not necessary to glance away from your audience for even a moment. This is truly the extemporaneous method. You know your material so well that you trust that you will present it effectively when the time comes. However, other speakers like to have the three-by-five cards ready to glance at, because they do serve to trigger your mind so well.

As you finish a particular section of your speech (when using the cue cards), you simply glance at the top of the next card and continue. Think of these cards as cue cards if you wish, or prompting cards.

Some speakers know their speeches so well that they rarely have to glance at the cards. But they may still have the cards there just in case.

Now here are the specific plus reasons for speaking this way:

- Because you know so well what you want to say, you don't have to worry about word order. Your presentation flows forward smoothly.
- Your presentation (the delivery of your speech) seems quite natural and not wooden, canned, or artificial.
- You don't have to worry about a loss of memory. Remember, you know your speech essentials so well that you can communicate the ideas and thoughts in a number of ways, if necessary, and as your own style and personality direct.
- You need have no fear of losing your place in a speech manuscript, because you don't have to bother with one. All you have is a stack of index cards with a lead line or phrase at the top of each one. Each card will *trigger* your memory to move to the next thought or topic.
- Should a better way of communicating a certain point suggest itself, or come to you while speaking, use it. You're not bound to a rigid structure or word-sentence order. In fact, this sometimes happens in the extemporaneous method. The result is a more effective and flexible presentation.
- Since you have only to glance at the lead line on each of your index cards, this method allows you to maintain excel-

lent eye contact with your audience. As a result, the overall quality of the communication is much higher.

- This method of speaking will give you a great deal of confidence and enthusiasm in your ability to make successful speeches.

When your speech is concluded, you have only to place the cards in order again to be ready to speak the next time.

The lead lines on your cards will establish grooves in your mind, and this is especially true if you give the same speech a number of times. After a number of presentations, you may not even need the index cards at all. And you may discover that you can present your speech in ever new and fresh ways. You just stand up and say it all in a new and interesting way each time.

How much better this method is than trying to trust your memory, reading the speech from a dull manuscript, or following a stilted, confined outline. This index card method allows room for *new* ways of saying the same thing. It's flexible. And it's certainly more enjoyable to speak this way. You can focus on the faces of your listeners and not have to keep looking away constantly.

I can vouch for this way of speaking. I've tried a full manuscript technique, an outline, and the memory and various notes routes. This method of lead phrases or lines on index cards is by far the best.

I hope you'll try this extemporaneous way of speaking, with or without the index cards as cues to trigger your mind. You'll like speaking this way, and your speeches will have a marvelously fresh and natural quality about them.

REVIEW POINTS FOR POWERFUL SPEAKING

- The extemporaneous method of speaking means advance preparation for a speech, but the exact way in which the material is communicated is more or less left open until the time of delivery.

- The extemporaneous method frees you from having to worry about word or sentence order.
- A lead line or phrase is written at the top of each three-by-five-inch index card. These lead lines serve as cues for triggering the mind, but the material itself is communicated as the style and personality of the speaker direct.
- The extemporaneous method naturally allows for a very high level of eye contact with the audience.

15

Strive for Voice Variety

Since your voice is the means by which you transmit the ideas and content of a speech, it is obviously quite important in the attainment of a high level of communication quality.

Some speakers can be irritating to listen to, because of a variety of vocal reasons:

1. The speaker mumbles. One reason this happens is simply because the speaker keeps his or her mouth nearly closed. You can prove it to yourself. Try to say something with your mouth almost shut. The result is a mumble.
2. The speaker's pace is too fast or slow. Speaking like you're rushed not only fails to get across to an audience; it leaves listeners bewildered from trying to follow you. On the other hand, a very slow rate of delivery becomes so monotonous that your audience may not be able to hold out until the bitter end. Try for a medium rate of delivery (with variety of course), but not too fast or slow.
3. The overuse of "and a" or "and er." This grates on the nerves of an audience. It may be a sign that the one doing the speaking didn't prepare for the speech or needs to develop more skill in presentation.
4. The purely boring voice is one with no life to it, no force, enthusiasm, or color. Such a voice makes members of an

audience wish they were anywhere but there, listening to the speech. A flat, dull, and cold voice creates boredom. As a speaker, you're not addressing the wall or an empty parking lot; the members of an audience have a *right* to expect your voice to be vibrant and warm.

5. Words and syllables become garbled by a speaker. Listeners want to hear the words and syllables of sentences uttered clearly and distinctly . . . not half omitted or snarled in transmission. Strive to beam them out to your audiences as clearly as possible.

VOICE VARIETY IS A MUST IN SPEAKING

There's no doubt about it. Voice variety helps to please an audience and make them want to keep listening to a speaker. Here are specific ways to get more variety in your own voice:

- Vary the rate of voice force you use.
- Vary your rate of delivery.
- Vary the pitch level of your voice. Try dropping your voice at appropriate times, and raising it in other places.

A voice can even do much to establish a certain kind of image. Actor Vincent Price believes this is why he has been cast so often in horror type films: "For some reason my voice has a timbre that evokes mystery, melodrama, and horror. I suppose the fact that I'm tall and speak with a theatrical voice contributes to my association with the occult."

In an article on the poetry reading of John G. Neihardt, Lucile F. Aly described the effects of his voice in public performances:

> He prolongs his vowels in stressed words, and his singing quality added dignity to the rhythm of the lines. His only training (for reading poetry aloud) was shouting poetry into the wind as he walked back roads in Nebraska. He understands well the value of

> a pause, and his excellent phrasing also included the much less common practice of increasing the rate on unimportant words after a pause. The combination of lengthened vowels, pauses, and quickened rate on unstressed words lended variety to the fairly long lines.

There's a way you can prove the importance of voice variety to yourself. For a solid week or longer, try saying everything in the same way, in the same tone, the same pitch level, and at the same rate or pace. You'll drive not only your friends and associates to distraction but also yourself. Audiences expect to hear variety and rightly so. Another way to prove this to yourself is to tape-record some speech material saying it all in the same way, the same rate, and tone level. Then listen back to it for as long as you can stand it. In fact, sometimes it really helps to record one of your speeches in a dull and lifeless way and listen back to it. Having heard it presented this way then helps you to make more of an effort to deliver it in a professional way.

TAPE – RECORDING YOUR SPEECH IS A DISCOVERY

I urge you without reservation to tape-record one or more of your speeches, when working on your presentation. Hearing what you sound like on tape (doing your best) will teach you a lot about what needs to be done to improve all aspects of your delivery. Each and every time you plan to present a speech, it would be smart to record the speech and then take notes on what you feel should be done to make it more effective.

By recording a speech several times, before its actual presentation before an audience, you can perfect many aspects of delivery and thus be much more prepared when the time comes to present it. Here are some other plus values of tape-recording a speech:

- If you've never heard your voice before on tape, it may

surprise you. A great many people have little or no idea what they actually sound like.

- Working with a tape-recorder allows you to hear the improvements you make in a speech (in the comparison of an early tape with a later one).
- It's easier to critique your own speech, because you, in effect, can assume the role of one listener in an audience.
- As you strive to improve as a speaker over a period of months and years, you can play back earlier taped speeches and actually realize the skills you're developing. This can be quite encouraging. This comparison is your proof that you're advancing as a speaker.
- Tape-recording helps to pin-point any voice defects, as well as other weaknesses of your overall speech (style, content, language, and so on).

THE BEAUTY OF PAUSES

Over the years, I've noted that most of the really fine speakers make very good use of pauses in their material. I realized this after listening to such dynamic speakers as Norman Vincent Peale, Adlai Stevenson, Billy Graham, Oral Roberts, and others. There's something very effective about a pause, when used in the right places in a speech. Here are some specific reasons for using a pause:

1. A pause will often dramatize the next thing you say. It puts a definite spotlight on your next sentence or idea.
2. A pause gives you a chance to catch your breath and collect your thoughts.
3. A pause can create a hushed or calming effect, allowing a significant point to register with an audience.
4. A pause often attracts fresh attention to you as the speaker. Use this as a technique, if you temporarily lose your audience's attention.

You can pick up additional ideas and tips on improving your voice, by listening more carefully to people on television, radio, in business meetings, and others you may hear in person. Here are just a few well-known people you can learn from, by listening to the variety they have in their voices:

1. David Brinkley
2. Vincent Price
3. Barbara Walters
4. Ronald Reagan
5. Tony Randall
6. Jessica Savage
7. Johnny Carson
8. Ted Kennedy
9. William Buckley
10. Roger Mudd
11. Dan Rather
12. Mike Wallace
13. John Chancellor

REVIEW POINTS FOR POWERFUL SPEAKING

- A speaker may grate on an audience's nerves by speaking too fast or too slow, using "and er" too much, mumbling, gargling words and syllables, or speaking with a dull and lifeless voice.
- Voice variety helps to please an audience and makes them want to keep listening to you.
- Tape-recording speeches can help you learn a great deal about your voice, delivery defects, and overall presentation.
- A great many people have little or no idea of what they sound like on tape.
- Comparing your earlier taped speeches with later, more

polished ones can be most encouraging, because it shows definite improvement.

- Use a pause to dramatize something in your speech, give yourself a chance to catch your breath, or allow the audience to re-focus attention on you and your speech.

16

The Sure Way to Become a Powerful Speaker

There is one definite way to increase your skill as a public speaker. In fact, there's no telling how far you might go as a speaker, by really applying the action step advised in this chapter. It could certainly lift you into the ranks of topnotch speakers one day.

What is this secret for masterful skill in public speaking? Actually it is no secret. It's quite simple. *Practice your speaking.* That's right. By practicing a great deal, you can greatly improve the quality of your speaking, and possibly become a truly dynamic speaker.

To practice effectively, really work on your speech. Each time you present it to your imaginary audience (or to a friend, or to your trusty tape recorder), concentrate. Try to improve your delivery.

There are people out there who would really like to be successful and powerful speakers, with all that it means in the way of money, success, prestige, and achievement. Then why don't they attain this goal? It's simple. They won't really practice enough to gain the necessary skill needed to be a fine speaker. Just as it's true in other fields, to reach the top or even come close to it as a public speaker, there's no escaping the basic need for plenty of practice.

But the more relevant point is that enough practice will make you a much more confident and capable speaker. Whatever your job or career field may be, being more at ease with the spoken word would pay off in a number of ways. To speak more effectively takes a lot of practice, growth, and development. The presentation skills of grabbing attention and holding it, introducing and concluding a speech, hitting home the main points, developing supporting materials (of the body of your speeches), voice variety, emotional appeals (if any), and the rest are all needed. In other words, few people will become champion speakers. But a great many (you included) can most certainly improve their overall speaking ability.

Even if a person is born with a gift or natural talent for speaking, it still requires a lot of practice and experience to become a champion in the field.

When a person stands before an audience, opens a full speech manuscript, and then reads all the material, it is not really communicating — at least on the high level many professionals shoot for. The person may be a good reader, but there's a difference between reading and speaking with your eyes on the audience. In my own mind, I've never thought of someone who reads an entire speech to be a speaker. That person may be called an oral reader, but not a speaker.

It's the hours and hours of practice. That's what separates the real pros from the mechanical and artificial speakers. "Practice makes perfect" is a very old cliché, but it is still very true — especially in public speaking.

In every college speech class I taught, there were always a number of students who would wait until the night before an assigned speech to prepare for it. Their last minute preparation often consisted of grabbing the current or past issue of *Reader's Digest,* in order to whip up a quick speech. Such a lack of preparation and interest was usually very obvious, and even the critiques from other students called their hand on this serious failure to practice and prepare sufficiently.

SOME REWARDS OF CONTINUOUS PRACTICE

Practicing the presentation of speeches brings a number of rewards, and they're well-worth noting here:

1. Practice increases your skill as a speaker, and enables you to deliver your speeches more effectively.
2. Practice builds your confidence as a speaker.
3. Practice helps you develop and present your material so the audience is likely to receive it better. And if the audience gets more from your speech, you're likely to come closer to achieving the purpose of your speech.
4. Practice makes the art of speaking far more interesting and enjoyable. You learn the techniques of presentation and how to move an audience, convince them, lead them to action, or whatever. To have an influence and effect on the lives of other people can be most stimulating indeed.
5. Practice which results in effective speeches improves your reputation as a speaker.
6. Practice improves your ability to communicate spontaneously. This can come in mighty handy all the way through life.
7. For those who become highly proficient speakers, practice can lead to a profitable career on the lecture circuit.

Lawyers, politicians, actors, and various national figures practice the speeches they give, because they know it helps them. By the same token, the more practice you can apply to your own speaking, the better speaker will you will become. Plenty of practice teaches you what is needed to hold an audience. It also keeps you enthused about your speeches, because you know you're ready to give an audience your best. Practice reveals the extra secrets and added touches already known by polished speakers. Speaking is like swimming, selling, painting, or whatever; the more you do it the better you usually become at it.

So however busy your schedule may be, take the time to work on your speaking delivery, your ability to get ideas across to an audience, and your overall communication quality. You are bound to grow, as a result of such practice. And you will most certainly develop into a very confident and effective public speaker.

REVIEW POINTS FOR POWERFUL SPEAKING

- Enough consistent practice presenting a speech can make you more confident and effective.
- There are no short-cuts to speaking power.
- Even if one is born with a gift or natural talent for speaking, it still requires a lot of practice and experience to become a topnotch speaker.
- Reading a speech before an audience is not really communicating.
- Enough practice on the presentation of your speeches makes your delivery much better received by an audience.
- Plenty of practice reveals the extra secrets and added touches of a polished speaker.

17

The Power of Sincerity in Speaking

If you think about the most powerful speeches you've heard in your lifetime, you'll agree that a major reason for their success was the sincerity of the speaker. Learn to put more sincerity into your speeches, and you'll be well on the road to masterful speaking.

Sincerity hits home with most listeners. Perhaps you feel that you have tried to be sincere in the speeches you may have already presented. But it's the degree of sincerity that's important. And the truth is that most speakers could be more effective, by doing some serious thinking about sincerity and then developing more of it in their speeches.

Sincerity can take you far in public speaking. Every good speaker projects genuine sincerity. The powerful, dynamic type of speaker has a great deal of it. And it gets across to audiences.

When French novelist Emile Zola spoke on February 21, 1898, to denounce the conspiracy against Captain Alfred Dreyfus, his speech was permeated with sincerity:

> Dreyfus is innocent. I swear it! I stake my life on it — my honor! At this solemn moment, in the presence of this tribunal which is the representative of human justice, before you, gentlemen, who are the very incarnation of the country, before the whole of France,

> before the whole world, I swear that Dreyfus is innocent. By my forty years of work, by the authority that this toil may have given me, I swear that Dreyfus is innocent. By all I have now, by the name I have made for myself, by my works, which have helped for the expansion of French literature, I swear that Dreyfus is innocent. May all that melt away, may my works perish, if Dreyfus be not innocent! He is innocent. All seems against me — the two Chambers, the civil authority, the most widely circulated journals, the public opinion they have poisoned. And I have for me only an ideal of truth and justice. But I am quite calm; I shall conquer. I was determined that my country should not remain the victim of lies and injustice. I may be condemned here. The day will come when France will thank me for having helped to save her honor.

THE SINCERITY APPEAL OF BILLY GRAHAM

Again, Billy Graham is a four-star example of the power of sincerity in action. The force behind Billy's tremendous appeal and attraction is no secret at all; a big part of his power is his great sincerity. "Sincerity is the biggest part of selling anything," says Billy. People who hear the evangelist speak may not always agree with his religious views and statements, but few doubt the man's sincerity . . . and that it is genuine.

Billy discovered the invaluable motivational power of sincerity one summer as a youth. He and a friend took their first jobs on their own, working as traveling salesmen for the Fuller Brush Company.

What happened was that Billy sold more brushes that memorable summer than any other salesman in the entire state of North Carolina. "I believed in the product." Believing in the subjects of your speeches will increase your sincerity when presenting material before audiences. Naturally if you believe in what you're saying, you're going to sound more sincere. It comes across to an audience. Strive to know the subjects of your speeches *intimately*, for it will definitely help you to project sincerity. Winston Churchill believed most deeply in the subjects of his speeches, and the statesman's strong sincerity came across. The sales manager of a given company believes in the product his or her sales team represents. So when that sales manager speaks to the members of the sales team, it sounds sincere because it *is* sincere.

Billy Graham did learn an important truth that summer in North Carolina. He learned the art of projecting his enthusiasm into the promotion of his product. In a similiar way, if you can learn to project your own enthusiasm into your speaking, you will succeed in accomplishing the purposes of your speeches. How you really feel about what you say in your speeches will get across sooner or later, especially if you present the same speech a number of times. The sincerity of a Churchill or a Billy Graham comes across in their voices, styles, and examples, which have a ring of heartfelt conviction and sincerity about them.

Turn back to the Zola speech section in this chapter and read it again. Even though you cannot hear his voice, there's a meaning, a substance, a gripping quality in the words and sentences themselves. Imagine what a powerful speech it must have been to hear on that day in 1898.

EVERY TRUE ORATOR HAS SINCERITY

Winston Churchill was a unique speaker with plenty of sincerity. People believed in him, and it was his great sincerity and determination in leading the British people through the dark days of World War II that made possible that nation's finest hour. Note Churchill's sincerity, when he presented his program in a speech on May 13, 1940:

> To form an administration of this scale and complexity is a serious undertaking in itself, but it must be remembered that we are in the preliminary state of one of the greatest battles in history, that we are in action at many points in Norway and in Holland, that we

> have to be prepared in the Mediterranean, that the air battle is continuous and that many preparations have to be made here at home. In this crisis I hope I may be pardoned if I do not address the House at any length today. I hope that any of my friends and colleagues, or former colleagues, who are affected by the political reconstruction, will make all allowance for any lack of ceremony with which it has been necessary to act. I would say to the House, as I said to those who have joined this Government: "I have nothing to offer but blood, toil, tears and sweat."

Daniel Webster's most famous speech was the *Reply to Hayne,* which filled some seventy-three printed pages. This speech was considered to be the most eloquent parliamentary address of Webster's era. It dealt with the right of the states to resist acts of Congress thought to be unconstitutional. Webster's sincerity, serious words, and deep-toned voice reached everyone in the Senate:

> When my eyes shall be turned to behold, for the last time, the sun in heaven, may I not see him shining on the broken and dishonored fragments of a once glorious Union, on States dissevered, discordant, on a land rent with civil feuds, or drenched, it may be, in fraternal blood. Let their last feeble and lingering glance rather behold the gorgeous ensign of the republic, now known and honored throughout the earth, still full high advanced, its arms and trophies streaming in their original lustre, not a stripe erased or polluted, nor a single star obscured, bearing for its motto, no such miserable interrogatory as, "What is all this worth?" nor those other words of delusion and folly, "Liberty first and Union afterwards," but everywhere, spread all over in characters of living light, blazing on all its ample folds, as they float over the sea and over the land, and in every wind under the whole heavens, that other sentiment, dear to every American heart, "Liberty and Union, Now and Forever, One and Inseparable."

Webster's audience was absolutely spellbound. Those who had heard him speak for three hours couldn't move—not because of the length or boredom but due to the power of the speech and the presentation. Almost all who heard the speech were caught up in the sincerity and emotion of his thoughts and words. Men cried. Others turned their heads to hide their emotion. Webster had done it again . . . really communicated . . . and it had moved his audience.

HOW TO GET MORE SINCERITY IN YOUR SPEECHES

Since genuine sincerity does so much to communicate to an audience, it's well worth the effort to instill more of it in your speaking. Here are some proven guidelines for getting more of this dynamic quality into your own speaking:

1. Use material in your speeches (key ideas, main ideas and points) that you really believe yourself. If you don't believe it, how can you expect an audience to do so?
2. Strive to project more enthusiasm in your overall presentation. Enthusiasm is contagious and often is equated with sincerity.
3. When you tape-record your speech (in practicing it), make sure your voice sounds sincere. Work on those sections or areas of the speech which don't seem to come across as genuine.
4. Be certain that you have some topnotch illustrations to help drive home your main ideas and points. Some high quality illustrations will definitely add to the heartfelt conviction and sincerity of your overall speech.
5. Strive to bring new light on the subject of your speech. Let your audience hear and feel in their hearts your effort and desire to uplift the truth and ennoble it.
6. Make your gestures as meaningful and genuine as possible.
7. Personalize some of your material, if the subject of your speech makes this possible. To personalize the material helps listeners to identify with it more.

8. Whenever you hear good sincerity in a speech, note how the speaker seemed to inject this quality into his or her speech.

REVIEW POINTS FOR POWERFUL SPEAKING

- A major reason for the success of a powerful speech is the speaker's projection of sincerity.
- Most speakers would benefit by getting more sincerity into their speeches.
- How a speaker really feels about the content of a speech is going to come across sooner or later, especially if the same speech is presented a number of times for different audiences.
- Voice, style, and specific examples can reveal sincerity.
- Every true orator has a great degree of sincerity.
- One way to get more sincerity into your speaking is to use material that you really believe, and topics you really feel strongly about.

18

the Victory of Helen Keller—She Kept Trying

Close your eyes and stop up your ears, and you'll get a small idea of what it's like to live in a sightless and soundless world. It's difficult to grasp the full meaning of it, for you know that you can see and hear.

There was no such assurance for the remarkable Helen Keller. In her dark and silent world, her soul cried out: "Light—give me light." She found that light and with it the will to become one of the great women of the twentieth century. She is a strong example that *impossible* is truly the adjective of fools. Our world today is a much brighter place, because this gentle lady came our way.

Her way was marked with obstacles almost from the start. Born a normal child, Helen Keller lost both her sight and hearing when just a baby of nineteen months. Doctors called it a "congestion of the brain and stomach." If you were blind and deaf in the 1880's, you were labeled an idiot. Yet, Helen Keller became a legend.

How did she do it? She learned to "see," though blind; she learned to "hear," though deaf. You may know people that are blind, or at least you've heard about them. Their blindness may have nothing to do with their eyes. Their eyes see, but the visual message is not transmitted to the brain. Helen Keller was blind but she had a level of understanding that many sighted people never achieve. George Bernard Shaw said about Helen Keller: "Would that all Americans could see as well as you." Something within her saw more clearly than we do with working eyes.

That something within Helen was unwilling to give up. But it had to be aroused. It was aroused by the person of Anne Sullivan Macy, who came to the Keller home to work with the young Helen. Anne was twenty then and partially blind herself. She'd entered Perkins Institution for the Blind in Boston and had been recommended to the Kellers by the Institution's director.

Presenting Helen with a doll, Anne took Helen's hand and manually spelled the word "d-o-l-l" onto it. This was the first word Helen had ever felt, for she had forgotten the few words she'd known before her illness. She was fascinated, but only because she thought it was a game. She was confused by what "d-o-l-l" was supposed to mean.

Some time later, Anne and Helen were at a water-pump. As the water rushed over Helen's fingers, Anne kept spelling "w-a-t-e-r." In a few moments, Helen understood and started spelling the word back. Wild with excitement, she then wanted the name for pump, the flowers, and especially Anne, her teacher.

This bright hope a teacher had brought her student was the beginning. Helen worked hard to learn through the sense of touch. For months and years, she practiced under the guidance of Anne. Each letter, syllable, and word she later spoke was learned through the sense of touch. She listened to speech by touching her fingers to the speaker's lips. To hear music, she placed her hand on the vibrating piano. In order to form the words of her teacher, she had to follow the movement of Anne's throat, lips, and tongue. Learning through touch opened the world to Helen, but not without years of practicing the sounds.

In this way, she learned to speak English, German, and French.

"Teacher." That's what Helen always called Anne. "Wonderful teacher" had made it all possible. No one ever loved a teacher more than Helen loved Anne Sullivan. Thanks to Anne, Helen became capable of making her way in life.

HELEN KELLER'S AMAZING ACCOMPLISHMENTS

Helen insisted on entering Radcliffe College in 1900. When President Wilson later asked her why she'd gone to Radcliffe, she replied: "Because they did not want me there. And I am stubborn and had made up my mind to go." Four years later she graduated with honors and world acclaim. She had decided to dedicate her life to helping the handicapped.

She helped plenty. One way was a two year vaudeville tour, not as a sensation, but as an impressive example for the blind and deaf. She knew they wanted a place in life, not pity. Appearing on the stage, she was saying in effect: "I'm blind and deaf, but look what I'm doing. You can do it too."

Transformed it. That's what Helen Keller did to vaudeville. She turned the theatre into a chapel. She and Anne were on the stage together. First Anne telling the story of how Helen learned to speak; how she'd made only meaningless noises until she was ten. Sarah Fuller, of the Horace Mann School for the Deaf in Boston, did much to develop Helen's speech, teaching her the basics. But Anne had continued the constant training for years. After telling a vaudeville audience all this, Anne would show them how she "spoke" into Helen's hand. Helen would then look at the audience, saying in clear tones, "I am not dumb now."

And she proved it too. She held her own with the likes of Oliver Wendell Holmes and Mark Twain. She met all the Presidents from the time of Teddy Roosevelt. She took her plea for the blind, deaf, and all handicapped to the town hall and lecture platform, inspiring courage and hope. She earned Doctor of Law degrees from both Glasgow University in Scotland and Witwatersrand in Johannesburg, South Africa. Wounded veterans in American war hospitals saw her shining faith. From her Westport, Connecticut, home, she helped many institutions and societies. Her essays and articles led the way in securing aid for the handicapped.

One story told often about Helen is about the time during the depression, when she raised $1 million for the American Foundation for the Blind. Given a $5,000 award for her work, she donated it, too.

When her beloved teacher died in 1936, Helen had to call for still more courage and faith. A long time friend, Polly Thomson, of Glasgow, Scotland, came to fill the void in her life.

Helen never forgot Anne. In her opening remark to handicapped students, she would say, "Good morning, boys and girls. I am happy to be with you if only for a little while. As my beloved teacher made my life bright and sweet, so shall your teachers blaze fresh trails for you for accomplishments and beauty of living." She filled children with wonder. Even after her hair began to gray, she continued speaking. Her voice was soft, at times indistinct, but those that heard her told of her inner radiance, her vivid expressive hands, the light in her eyes, her smiling face. She reached her audience and enriched their lives.

When President Eisenhower met her, he could not hold back the tears. But when she touched his face with her fingertips, so she might see him in her way, he smiled for her.

The Bible helped Helen to smile. It was the book that influenced her most. She believed that God is within man and that life does have meaning. "I believe life is given us so we may grow in love, and I believe that God is in me as the sun is in the color and fragrance of a flower— the light in my darkness, the voice in my silence."

REMEMBER HELEN KELLER IN YOUR OWN LIFE AND WORK

Within her dark and silent world, Helen Keller found light and the power to conquer her handicap. She taught us much about faith and the human art of trying. She proved that what limits man is man himself.

Her own words are a fitting guide for a courageous life of success and victory over all obstacles: "If you try to do something good every day to someone else, you will keep happy and find life great and beautiful."

Helen Keller is a real example for anyone interested in improving their speaking. Blind and deaf, she started with overwhelming handicaps but still rose above them to become an inspiring speaker who traveled the world to address audiences. As you strive to upgrade your own speaking ability, keep her example in mind.

19

P.T. Barnum's Sure-Fire Recipe for Success

This rest of this chapter contains a speech I have given, and which you can use as an example. It is a speech that informs, persuades, entertains, and also inspires. The speech is based on the code for success in life left by that illustrious promoter of the last century P. T. Barnum. Barnum has caught the imagination of the modern era. There is currently a smash hit broadway show called simply "Barnum."

Barnum's pointers for success are so important and of such interest to audiences that most of them are covered in the speech. Some of them could be combined, in order to reduce the number of these tips presented.

Be sure to note the examples, anecdotes, and quotes from Barnum, himself, which form the supporting materials for the speech. This has proved to be a successful speech for me, and audiences have responded to it warmly.

P. T. Barnum was known as the greatest American showman of his day. When he died in 1891, the *London Times* called him "that fine flower of western civilization, that arbiter elegantiarum to Demos, who gave a luster to America. His name is a proverb already, and proverb it will continue."

Barnum left what he personally felt was a sure-fire recipe for success. He believed that if one would follow the rules he discovered and practiced himself, that person would achieve substantial success in his or her chosen work and in life.

At the young age of nineteen, Barnum founded and edited a newspaper in Danbury, Connecticut. This personal effort enabled him to show his interest in politics, and his *Herald of Freedom* newspaper brought him to public notice. Throughout his life, Barnum often wrote for syndicates and magazines on various subjects. Much of his time was also spent lecturing, his main lecture being "The Art of Money-Getting."

In 1844, Barnum toured England and Europe. He brought the famous Jenny Lind, the "Swedish Nightingale," to America in 1850. Largely through his skillful promotion, Jenny became a front page celebrity who grossed nearly a million dollars at the nation's box offices. That was quite a fortune in those days.

Offered the Democratic nomination for governor of Connecticut, in 1852, Barnum declined but later ran for Congress, though he was defeated. In the 1870's, he opened his "Greatest Show on Earth" in Brooklyn and enjoyed great success with it. His museum, menagerie, and circus required some five hundred men and horses for transporting.

Barnum's circus later merged with that of J. A. Bailey to form the Barnum and Bailey Circus. Barnum used an imported elephant named Jumbo for his show. He seemed to have a sixth sense as to what audiences would enjoy.

Called the "Magician of Mirth," "The Lord of Laughter and Fun," "The Dispenser of Amusement," and "The Prince of Humbugs," P. T. Barnum loved his popularity. He followed a very strict idea or rule book of showmanship, always giving the public more than it paid for and keeping his shows free from all indecencies.

Barnum thought that the common man deserved amusement for his spare time—entertainment that was wholesome and non-corrupting. Known as the father of modern day publicity, he created the popular museum and turned tent carnivals into the modern three-ring circus.

The illustrious showman did a lot of work for the city of Bridgeport, Connecticut. Its beautiful Seaside Park was a gift from him. He also laid out many streets of the main city and planted seventeen thousand trees. A beautiful fountain was placed in a park in front of a church. Eventually, he owned more than three hundred buildings.

Barnum often said he couldn't live in a town without trying to improve it. He served as mayor of Bridgeport from 1875 to 1876.

He was sunny and alive at all times, with an inborn desire to make people happy. He went to great lengths to thrill children and often fixed the prices and days to be more convenient for them. No matter where he went, he always had a cheerful word for everyone. His presence at one of his shows was enough to usually greatly increase the box office take.

A showman to the end, his last words when he died in Philadelphia were a request to know the day's receipts of the circus. In 1907, his circus was sold to the Ringling Brothers.

Great success that he was, Barnum followed his own code book of rules. He often passed these rules along to others who sought success. Here is his master list of action steps for real success:

1. *Select the vocation which is most congenial to your tastes.*

Millions have to literally drag themselves to work each day, because they made a wrong vocational choice. Take stock of your situation. If you're in the wrong kind of work or career, start making plans now to leave it as soon as you can for work more to your liking. Life goes by fast enough anyway. You might just as well be doing work you're suited for and like.

2. Learn something useful to fall back on, if things don't go the way you hope and plan.

Having worked as a grocery store clerk after grammar school, the first thing P. T. did after moving to New York, in 1834, was to open such a store. Eight years later, when a New York museum went on sale, Barnum managed to open it as his own Barnum's American Museum. He had natural ability as a promoter, but he was also learning more about skill every day — the skills of showmanship. In the years that followed, his name became as important as the attractions he so well presented and promoted.

Barnum's promotional abilities and knowledge paid off for the rest of his life, but his grocery clerk experience was always something he could fall back on if necessary. This is still a very sound course of action for the unpredictable 1980's and 1990's.

3. Whatever you do, do it with all your might. If you have to, work at your goal both early and late. Put your whole self into it.

Perhaps the best way to think of this idea of commanding all your might and powers is to view it as *determination.* A determined person is a powerful individual. Boxing immortal Jim Corbett was determined to defeat the great John L. Sullivan in the historic fight held in New Orleans on September 7, 1892. The purse was for $25,000 (a lot of money then), but Corbett was so sure he would win that he also placed a side bet on himself for $10,000.

When the bell sounded, Corbett began to dodge Sullivan and kept on doing it. Quickly sidestepping the champion, Corbett broke Sullivan's nose. Sullivan roared, "Come in and fight!"

But Corbett refused. For twenty rounds this continued, unitl Corbett realized that Sullivan was ripe for the kill. Corbett's main strategy was simply to avoid Sullivan's rushes with style, while continually getting in counter punches. Corbett knocked the champion out in twenty-one rounds.

Corbett held the title for the next four years, and his victory over Sullivan remained the greatest achievement of his life. It made him a man of international importance overnight. His advice for more successful and happier living is worth remembering and following: "When you're weary from trying, don't quit; fight one more round. That one more round may make all the difference and bring you success." It should also be said that it usually takes a determined person to fight one more round, go the distance, and attain an objective or goal.

4. Exercise both caution and boldness. Before rushing into some project, try to determine your chances of success.

Too much caution is of course dangerous, and the same is true of too much boldness. While exercising both caution and boldness, depend on your own personal exertions. Students who earn academic degrees learn this fortunately at a fairly early age. They know they have to stay in there and keep plugging away at the books to get their degrees. Trusting and depending on your own personal efforts can pay off in better jobs, advanced degrees, more money, and all kinds of personal accomplishment.

5. Don't let the horror of the blues or depression take over you.

Barnum advised everyone to fight back. Fight the blues with all your might, for depression and the blues can wreck your plans and wipe out your enthusiasm.

There's a definite way to send the blues packing every time. Whenever a negative thought seems to try to dominate you, do your best to filter it out. This takes mental discipline at first, but if you continue allowing only good and positive thoughts to enter, the blues will depart for other weaker minds.

6. Be systematic. Have the time and place for everything.

One proven method for a better daily organization is to make a list each night of the things you must do the next day, to keep advancing and moving towards your goals and the success you seek. Then simply do the things you have listed each day. When you make out your list, whether it's for the next day or week, strive to put the items down in order of their importance. This will help to assure that you get the priority items done first.

Barnum made it his business to always have time for reading, and he said that it is a definite must for true success. He learned of the sale of the New York museum while reading a newspaper. Opening it as his own American Museum was an important step in his career, because it led to better things later. Countless ideas that have led many to eventual success and fortune have come from the daily reading of magazines and newspapers. The same is true for books.

7. Let money work for you.

A growing savings account is money working for you. It may come in handy when you least expect it. When an opportunity presents itself, having a cash reserve can often mean the chance to take advantage of it. Putting money to work can also mean investments. Not everyone has the extra funds to invest. If and when you do, with sound judgement, you might earn a handsome profit or even build a small to large fortune. Big entertainment names like Steve Allen, the late Bing Crosby, Gene Autry, Dana Andrews, and others all made a large part of their fortunes through wise and fortunate investments. Your money has little chance of growing if it's hoarded. It takes money to make more money.

8. Advertise your business.

Barnum strongly believed in this rule and followed it regularly in his own life and work.

If P. T. Barnum, expert showman and promoter that he was, believed in advertising in the 1870's, you can quickly see how vital it is today in building up a business. When Barnum realized that his own fame was a major factor in his success, he fully exploited his name in promoting his circus. He has been compared to Shakespeare for his advertising eloquence. The reported author of statements like "there's a sucker born every minute," Barnum drew a sharp line between innocent humbug and outright fraud.

It must be added here that Barnum thought that few persons can become masters of many varied interests. He left a warning along these lines: "Do not scatter your powers. Stick to one kind of business only, until you succeed or experience shows you must abandon it."

When P. T. Barnum died in 1891, he was a Harotio Alger hero in the real meaning of the words. His own last words were about the business he built from the ground up and loved so much. Reported to be worth $5 million when he died, he was also a very rich man in friends, family, and a sense of worthwhile achievement. His life and career brought entertainment and happiness to millions of people.

P. T. Barnum's magic recipe for success is certainly valid and right on target for today's modern era. Remember his rules as you plan and build your own success. His recipe can and will help you make success a reality in your own work and life.

20

Questions and Answers to Guide You

Here are the most frequently asked questions and answers about the art of public speaking, getting started, increasing your confidence and effectiveness, and so on. These questions and answers are meant to offer guidance and encouragement for your own speaking:

Q. How much money do speakers make?
A. It depends on how many times they speak each year and the size of the fees. Some well-known speakers receive $8,000 and more for a single speaking engagement. A big name and national celebrity like Bob Hope or Johnny Carson reportedly receives $40,000 for a speaking date. Many new and unknown speakers, who book themselves, charge as little as $75 or $100 for speaking at schools and colleges (plus transportation expenses or gas mileage). Their fee goes up from $100 to several hundred and more, if they speak for a major club, business group, or national association. The size of the fee you can charge depends on how much experience you have, who the speaking is done for, how much in demand your topic or program is, how far you have to travel to keep the engagement, and whether you offer any special features in your program.

Once you become in demand, it can mean several thousand dollars and more every time you speak.

Q. How long does a new speaker have to work on a free basis?
A. Some enterprising speakers start receiving fees from the start. Much depends on how badly you need the experience and whether a school, college, group, or club really wants the program you're offering (or perhaps believes they might get you free).

Q. Certain speakers I hear from time to time are very difficult to follow. Why is this so, when others are most interesting?
A. Unfortunately, some speakers have not learned to *say* what they *mean*. They may not communicate or get across to an audience.

Q. What is the best way to introduce a speech?
A. Opinions vary. Some believe that a reference to the occasion for the speech is good. Others say the use of an example leading into the subject is most effective. Still other views include paying the audience a compliment, stressing the importance of the subject, or identifying with the audience in some way. I think it's helpful to experiment with different types of introductions. In this way, you'll sooner or later find the best introduction for a given speech. Sometimes just a direct opening statement works well. Here's an example from a speech on being a bolder and more enterprising person:

> It takes boldness to get through this life. It often takes a bold person to confront today's income tax forms, to get married or divorced, to go into military service, fight a battle, have an operation, support a family, build a successful career, make a speech, and so on down a long line of various lifetime actions.

Q. Gestures worry me when speaking. Can you tell me what to do with my hands?
A. Rather than use the same gestures, try instead for a variety.

Generally speaking, use small gestures when speaking to a small audience and wide or big ones when addressing a large crowd. If most of the members of your audience are on the young side, use a plentiful number of gestures. A younger audience generally likes to see more gestures, although there's no binding rule on it.

Q. What is impromptu speaking?
A. It shows a speaker the difficulty of speaking without preparation. Improptu speaking is getting up and sounding forth on a given subject with no time to prepare at all. It's spur-of-the-moment speaking. It can be a useful exercise, in learning how to evaluate the vocal and communication habits of a speaker.

Q. Can you give a definition of an ideal orator?
A. Cicero, perhaps the greatest orator of all time, once gave his definition of the ideal orator: "In an orator, the acuteness of the logicians, the wisdom of the philosophers, the memory of lawyers, the voice of tragedians, the gesture almost of the best actors, is required. Nothing, therefore, is more rarely found among mankind than a consummate orator." I find it hard to improve on this definition.

Q. How can I find a suitable subject for a speech?
A. Asking yourself a variety of questions can often lead to the right speech subject. Here are some examples of such questions: (1) What national, regional, or local issues am I personally interested in? (2) Is there a possible subject in the travel I've done? (3) What are some of my major interests in life? (4) Do I enjoy reading fiction or non-fiction? The kind of reading you like best may hold a clue for a subject. (5) What clubs, social groups, or business organizations do I belong to? Is there a spinoff idea for a speech there?

Q. What is "audience feedback?"
A. The reactions of an audience let a speaker know what kind

of communication is taking place. If some listeners in the audience, for example, appear to be straining to hear, it may mean that you aren't talking loud enough. Other signs from an audience are puzzled looks, listeners who look away, frowns, and nods of agreement.

Q. What should a speaker do when he or she forgets what comes next?
A. Try to stay in control of the situation. Don't panic. A long pause is okay (if not too long) and can give you a chance to recover and get back on the track of your speech. If you know the ideas and content of your speech well enough, you could paraphrase the material; say it in a different way but still your own. If you know the thoughts behind the words, it's always possible to transmit the material in a variety of ways. Another option is to summarize what you've already said. While doing so, you can decide in your mind how to proceed from there.

Q. What are the major benefits of a college course in public speaking?
A. The most valuable benefit is the experience you'll gain in speaking before the rest of the class. The more speeches and presentations you're required to give in a course, the better it will prove to be. Other very helpful benefits are learning how to choose a suitable speech subject, discovering the skills of delivering a speech, planning, outlining, and writing a speech, and finding out about the various branches of speech communication.

Q. How can I cope with this fear of speaking I've always had?
A. Just be prepared as best you can. Know your speech material so well that you have confidence in it and yourself. Know also that you have worthwhile material that will help the audience in some way (inform, entertain, inspire, or persuade them). Breathing deeply before speaking seems to help a lot of ner-

vous speakers. As for the long run, I believe the best cure for the fear of speaking comes from experience before an audience.

Q. I often have trouble deciding how to end a speech. What advice can you offer?
A. Try to find the best way to tie it all together. Sometimes an illustration or strong quotation will do it. Seek to bring your presentation to a logical and satisfying ending. As a strong example, here is how Winston Churchill concluded an action speech, by using the rhetoric of repetition, a poetic device:

> We shall not flag nor fail. We shall go on to the end, we shall fight in France, we shall fight on the seas and oceans, we shall fight with growing confidence and strength in the air, we shall defend our island, whatever the cost may be, we shall fight on the beaches, we shall fight on the landing grounds, we shall fight in the fields and in the streets, we shall fight in the hills, we shall never surrender.

Q. Can the study of public speaking be of help in choosing the right vocation?
A. Most definitely. I majored in speech communication in college, and it was during this time that I realized that I wanted to spend my life in some branch of communications. My study of speech and public speaking pointed me in the right direction. It propelled me into the right arena. It has done the same for many others. In a class on beginning debate, which I helped teach at Murray State University, two college seniors "found" themselves. They became enormously interested in debate (one branch of speech communication) and took part in the entire debate competition (including tournaments) for the year. They won some major debates with students from other universities. Near the end of the term, these two graduating seniors told the rest of us that they were going on to law school and that the debate course had made them realize that this was what they wished to do.

Q. I can't decide between two different subjects for a speech. What should I do?
A. Think about the way you would handle each subject. Which subject do you feel you could handle most effectively? Then, too, one of the subjects may be better suited for your audience. Consider the *occasion* of the speech, if any, and some of the facts about your audience (education level, general age, their interest in the subject). In other words, examine each subject in view of your audience. Thinking about your audience and the way you would handle each subject will help you reach the right decision.

Q. Does reading a speech out loud help to learn the material (when preparing)?
A. I certainly think so. It helps to establish the pattern of ideas and thoughts in your mind. Along with reading the material out loud, it's also a great help to tape-record the speech and listen to it a number of times.

Q. What is the proper thing to do, when and if a few listeners in an audience continue to talk and whisper while a speech is being presented?
A. I've seen speakers in this situation get good results from a long pause, while looking intently at the two listeners who are talking. Sometimes a dramatic or surprising (even startling) statement will work, providing your material includes it.

Humor is often the best way out of any awkward situation. I once saw a fine entertainer handle some rude members of an audience. One evening in a Reno, Nevada, casino showroom, singer Tony Martin was performing a wonderful medley of top song hits. Just below the stage, a man sitting with several others at a table kept blowing cigarette smoke right up into Tony's face. It got so bad in the middle of one song that Tony was almost totally engulfed in a cloud of smoke. Having put up with it as long as he could, Tony looked down at the man and quipped, "Don't you ever inhale?"

Q. I've been out of school for years, but I'm thinking about sitting in on a college class in public speaking. Would I feel out of place as a regular student in the class?
A. Not at all. An increasing number of adults are returning to the college classroom. Many are in their middle or even senior years. Continuing education is quite popular these days. During my university teaching years, my department chairman asked me to teach an adult class in basic public speaking. Since all those who wanted to take the course worked during the day, the class was held each Monday night for two hours, with a short break in the middle. This was one of my very best classes. These older adult students were very interested in developing their communication skills and put a lot of time and effort into the class. A number of them achieved an effective speaking delivery.

Q. Which type of speech is the most difficult to present?
A. This is a matter of opinion. Many believe that the speech to entertain is the hardest, because it can be difficult to amuse an audience. In my own mind, I believe that the speech to persuade often proves to be the most difficult. This is especially true, if the views, ideas, and beliefs of the audience are stubbornly held and therefore hard to change or influence.

Q. Is the subject of a speech more important than the person who presents it?
A. No. I would say that the speaker is just as important. One may have a marvelous subject for a speech, but if the material is not effectively presented, much of the potential subject value will be lost.

Q. The last speaker I heard looked at his watch several times during the speech. Wasn't this poor judgement?

A. Never look at your watch when presenting a speech. If you're well-prepared, you'll know the time sequence necessary for various sections of your speech. Some speakers place a watch (with a large dial) on the lectern beside their notes, for quick time checks. This is a good idea.

Q. What pleases an audience most in a speaker and subject matter?
A. Audiences vary of course, but generally speaking most of them want to hear something they can talk about later to their friends or family members. New information pleases them, because it lets them come away with the feeling that they've learned something. Funny or interesting stories are popular, and the same goes for provocative ideas. Actually there are many things that can please an audience. If you communicate your own strong interest and excitement about your material, your audience will tend to feel that their time was well spent listening to your speech.

Q. What is meant by integrity of a speaker?
A. As a speaker, you're expected to do the necessary advance preparation for presenting an effective speech. Audiences have the right to expect professional material, or at least speeches that are worthwhile and presented as well as possible.

21

Ideas for Immediate Speech Projects

This chapter covers ideas for a variety of speech topics. The subjects are broken down into a number of areas for faster and easier reference. Each listing also gives a suggested partial introduction for the topic. Whenever you're stumped for a likely speech topic, you can turn to this chapter and look over these possible choices:

1. Interest area — education
   Type of speaker — school teacher, educator, PTA member
   Topic of speech — "What Matters Most in Education — the Teacher or the Subject?"
   Partial introduction — "It's the supreme art of the teacher to awaken joy in creative expression and knowledge," said the brilliant Albert Einstein. Much like the old question that still haunts many in the marketing profession (salesman or the product?), what about the world of teaching? Just which is the most important? Is it the teacher or the subject that matters most?"

2. Interest area — management
   Type of speaker — managers or supervisors (or someone interested in management)
   Topic of speech — "Managing People Well Is an Art"
   Introduction — "Can anyone be a manager? Is manage-

ment skill something that any responsible person with business experience can learn or develop? The answer to both questions, as you might expect, is a flat no. Anyone who really explores the who, what, when, why, and how of management will realize that the ability to supervise and manage people effectively is a definite art."

3. Interest area — raising children
   Type of speaker — a parent
   Topic of speech — "Children Need Discipline in Their Formative Years"
   Introduction — "There are basic theories today on raising children. One voiced by a number of authorities is not to inhibit the child in almost any way — to let him or her do practically anything. The other major view is that children cannot be brought up without discipline. If they are, the parents will find, like so many already have, that their children have become spoiled and selfish by their teens."

4. Interest area — youth leadership
   Type of speaker — youth counselor
   Topic of speech — "What Today's Youth Leaders Need the Most."
   Introduction — "Perhaps the one word that best describes today's young people is "searching." The youth of today may not be quite as restless as those of the mid 1960's were, but high school and church youth department groups are filled with many young persons trying to find themselves and something — an idea, cause, or belief that will challenge their interest and enthusiasm."

5. Interest area — love and marriage
   Type of speaker — a married person (or marriage counselor)
   Topic of speech — "The Trouble With Too Many Marriages"

Partial introduction — "One valuable and dynamic quality that can make your marriage more successful and also much happier is an increased sense of humor. It can work wonders in a great many marriages. English writer Thomas Hood summed up the value of humor most effectively: "The sense of humor is the just balance of all the faculties of man, the best security against the pride of knowledge and the conceits of the imagination, the strongest inducement to submit with a wise and pious patience to the vicissitudes of human existence."

6. Interest area — selling, salesmanship
   Type of speaker — sales manager or member of a sales team
   Topic of speech — "Your Two Most Vital Sales"
   Partial introduction — "You make sales every work day, at least preferably. Some are big sales and others not so large. When you really think about it, no two sales you make are exactly alike. In one sale, you may have more objections of the prospect to overcome. In another sale, you just don't seem to communicate as effectively as you wish. In reality, every sales professional sells three things, and you must too: Yourself, your ideas, and your product or service. The first two are the most vital sales you ever make."

7. Interest area — music
   Type of speaker — musician, music historian, or general lover of music
   Topic of speech — "William C. Handy: Man With a Dream"
   Partial introduction — "At sundown each evening at a park in Memphis, Tennessee, a familiar tune is heard in memory and tribute to a great composer. A clock in St. Louis chimes the same melodic strains in his honor. In Florence, Alabama, students study in a school named

after this same composer. Why so much fanfare and honor for one man? Because, in his courageous journey from Alabama to New York City, he scaled the starry heights of the world of popular music, leaving behind his footsteps many a heart that would beat just a little faster to the thrill of his music. Yes. William Handy's story is still more vivid proof that you have to dream big."

8. Interest area — ESP and the occult
   Type of speaker — anyone interested in the concept of reincarnation
   Topic of speech — "If Reincarnation Is the Plan — There's No Escape"
   Partial introduction — "The idea of reincarnation, or continuous rebirth, is fascinating to think about. Many believe this is the plan for mankind. If it is, one thing seems clear. There's no escape. Sooner or later, all of us will have to pay for any and all bad things done in previous lives.

   "To accept reincarnation is to believe that each one of us returns again and again to earth. In fact, according to this ancient concept of rebirth, all of us are in reality old souls. We've all been here many times before."

9. Interest area — variation on the occult
   Type of speaker — anyone interested in ghost research and mystery in general
   Topic of speech — "Visiting Ghosts"
   Partial introduction — "Ghosts in the White House? Say it isn't so. I'm afraid it's true. Not only do ghosts visit the famous house on Pennsylvania Avenue; they are seen at times by the living. Something, for example, is evidently keeping the ghost of Abraham Lincoln restless. Reported sights of his ghost in the White House have increased in recent years. Some reports have claimed that the ghost of Lincoln still prowls the second floor of the White

House near the historic Lincoln bedroom. Over the years, this is the one area where the ghost has been seen the most."

10. Interest area — inspiration
    Type of speaker — teacher or anyone interested in inspiring an audience via a historical subject
    Topic of speech — "Earth's D-Day"
    Partial introduction — "It was fifteen minutes past midnight. Not far from five beaches lay the greatest fleet of warships the world had ever known. The gray, murky light gave hints of the approaching dawn. The day had finally arrived. It would be a day of pain and death. It would be a day of courage and bravery, but also one of fear. Most of all, the long day ahead would be stamped and filed in the memory of the human heart; a day destined for the pages of human history."

11. Interest area — patriotism
    Type of speaker — anyone who believes in promoting patriotism across the land.
    Topic of speech — "The Magnificence of America"
    Partial introduction — "This is a speech about America, still the greatest land on earth by far. You hear a lot of negative things about this country, our problems, the uncertain economy, inflation, crookedness in high places, and so on. But one fact remains. Most of the heavy traffic is still one way — into this country."

12. Interest area — the mountains
    Type of speaker — anyone interested in travel, the mountains, tourism
    Topic of speech — "The Lure of the Great Smoky Mountains"
    Partial introduction — "Once you see them, you never forget them. The sight of a dawn or a sunset over these

mountains is captured forever in the photographic storehouse of your mind's memory. If you're fortunate enough to live near them, you count yourself blessed. Near to them or far, though, there's no escape from the lure of the great Smoky Mountains."

13. Interest area — retirement
Type of speaker — a senior citizen or retired person (or retirement association official)
Topic of speech — "Retirement: Your Finest Hours"
Partial introduction — "Your retirement years will be what you make them. A keen spirited man crossed the Pacific in his boat a few years ago for the second time. He was sixty when he crossed the first time, seventy the second time. He looks forward to his third trip when he'll be eighty. Retirement for him is just fresh opportunity.

"The ocean may lure some, but there is enough land-oriented activity to keep you busy and interested for a dozen lifetimes. The point to keep in mind is that active, zestful, enthusiastic, and creative use of your time is a darn sight more exciting than a rest in the cow pasture."

14. Interest area — the insurance industry
Type of speaker — life insurance agent, insurance sales manager, public relations officers of insurance companies
Topic of speech — "Little Things Mean a Lot to Policy-Holders"
Partial introduction — "Talk about satisfied clients. A local insurance agent has a good part of the surrounding area on his policy-holder list and owes a great deal of his success to the chorus phrase of a past hit record called 'Little Things Mean a Lot.'

"Every policy-holder receives the same velvet service. When the policy is sold, it's just the beginning. This agent keeps in touch, frequently, offering to change the mode of premium payment, to change the dividend election, to inform his clients on a new option, a new plan, or a benefit available to them."

15. Interest area — success motivation — getting ahead
Type of speaker — company officers, group, section, department, or plant leaders, and various others
Topic of speech — "Your Drive to Succeed Is Invaluable"
Partial introduction — "Someone once said that 'success is within you.' There was even a book written about it. The personal resources that you draw on to succeed are indeed within your own self. At the top of the list of these vital resources is one known simply as drive-power. Your drive to succeed is a must. It's invaluable to all areas of your success.

"Millions of people the world over are caught up in this same drive to get ahead. This drive-power is the fuel that gets results, the substance that backs your daily purpose, and the generating source of energy that keeps you on the beam and moving toward your next goal."

16. Interest area — the arena of politics
Type of speaker — student or adult interested in the burdens of today's taxpayer
Topic of speech — "Life as a Congressman: Christmas Every Day"
Partial introduction — "With the yearly grab-bag of financial goodies automatically theirs, most congressmen do all in their power to stay on the Potomac. Members of Congress just seem to keep getting richer, while most United States taxpayers keep trying to pay for it all.

"Going to Congress is certainly a sure way to a fortune, compared to the lot of most Americans. It's easy to see why those who try it (to get elected) — who go for the roses — like it so well after they've been on the Hill awhile. The congressional halls are literally made of gold."

17. Interest area — music entertainment
Type of speaker — travel promoters, agents, choir leaders, and others interested in choir music
Topic of speech — "The Most Famous Choir in the World"
Partial introduction — "Millions have heard and marveled at the Mormon Tabernacle Choir. Visitors journey from all over the world to Salt Lake City to see the sights at Temple Square and hear this most famous choir in the world. Acoustics in the huge tabernacle are unexcelled, according to noted artists like Eugene Ormandy. The tabernacle was first used in 1867.

"The great choir has been invited to sing all over the world. In 1955, it performed in a string of European cities. There was standing room only, wherever the choir appeared. British critics were lavish with praise: 'Outstandingly beautiful, with ethereal purity of effect,' said the *London Times*. The weekly tabernacle broadcast is carried over radio stations all over America, on shortwave, and also on the Armed Forces Radio Network. Over eight hundred stations release its radio-television program each week. Gold records have been awarded the choir for two albums."

18. Interest area — personal growth
Type of speaker — student, parent, teacher, counselor, business person, housewife
Topic of speech — "The Power of Discipline"
Partial introduction — "Discipline is one of the most powerful things in the world. You can definitely develop more of it, and that's why I'm here today. Why is discipline so vital? Because it gets things done. It can certainly

accomplish wonders in your life and help you send the blues packing. With enough discipline at your control, you can launch your own business, make more money, find greater happiness, complete a special course of study, improve your personality, get a better job, and bring new vistas of success into your life."

19. Interest area — inspiration — personal motivation
Type of speaker — businessman, student, others who believe in making dreams come true
Topic of speech — "The Dream Oral Roberts Made Come True"
Partial introduction — "College president, minister, and evangelist Oral Roberts announced back in 1960 that he was going to build a university. A pastureland of some five hundred acres in Tulsa, Oklahoma was surveyed and eventually turned into a modern and thriving university.

"At the time Roberts announced his plans to build a great university, many in the Tulsa area said that one man couldn't do it. 'States and cities build universities — not evangelists,' they said. But Oral Roberts went right ahead, putting up the first buildings in 1962."

20. Interest area — adventure, travel, treasure-hunting
Type of speaker — anyone interested in travel, adventure
Topic of speech — "Looking for Diamonds in Arkansas"
Partial introduction — "How many trips have you taken with the chance to go home with one or more diamonds? Whether they find any diamonds or not, millions of Americans visit the famous Crater of Diamonds in Arkansas and have the time of their lives.

"It's a lot of fun to spend an afternoon turning up dirt, in hopes of finding a real diamond. What if your back does begin to ache after a few hours of bending over? You're looking for anything that seems to glitter. That dirt you're standing on and sifting through might just turn out to be pay dirt."

21. Interest area — personal development
Type of speaker — parent, student, manager, business person
Topic of speech — "The Satisfaction of Achievement"
Partial introduction — "Life has many blessings, but one that belongs near the top of the list is the satisfaction of achievement. Something deep within most of us longs for fulfillment and continually urges us to excel, to go for the roses, to make our mark in the world, and in so doing, to perhaps make the world a better place in which to live."

22. Interest area — nostalgia
Type of speaker — anyone with an interest in the old popular songs of yesterday
Topic of speech — "Funny How the Great Old Songs Get to You"
Partial introduction — "Nostalgia has been quite the rage in recent years. And one of the direct ways in which the memories of the past and the great popular singers come rolling back is via the great old songs of yesterday.

"These still-wonderful songs of bygone years grab you by the ear and the heartstrings too. Hearing them again is like saying hello to old friends. Just today at lunch, a cafeteria organist played a medley of 'Lady of Spain,' 'It Had to Be You,' 'Tea for Two,' and 'To Each His Own.' It was wonderful to hear these familiar tunes again."

23. Interest area — survival
Type of speaker — student, historian, teacher
Topic of speech — "The Challenge of Nature"
Partial introduction — "Every time a fair-sized storm hits town, you hear people voicing their worries and complaints. The shelter, good protection, and a dry

place to sleep at night, are all usually taken for granted. What if we didn't have them? What if we had to endure some of the incredible hardships faced and overcome by the early American colonists? Having to toughen up might be good for us. How would we have faced the same challenge? Hopefully, head on and with courage."

24. Interest area — marketing, business
Type of speaker — sales manager, sales representative, company officer, store owner
Topic of speech — "People Still Love to Be Sold"
Partial introduction — "One basic truth about the world of selling needs to be sounded again and again — the stimulating fact that prospects, customers, and people in general still love to be sold; they love to see a good sales person in action and to do business with that kind of sales representative.

"People enjoy being sold on all levels too. Take the thousands of products sold in drug stores, department stores, variety, specialty, and other stores. Many customers don't like to be rushed or to have to wait on themselves. Many of today's stores are losing lots of sales, because someone decided it might be better to let customers find what they want and bring it to a check-out counter. It's not better, according to the many expressions of complaints. A great many of the buying public dislike the new self-service practice."

25. Interest area — nature, the great outdoors
Type of speaker — any lover of the great outdoors
Topic of speech — "The Return of Spring"
Partial introduction — "It's in the air. That wonderful fresh smell and feeling, almost a tingle inside you, that draws you like a virtual magnet to the magic world of the

great outdoors. With a new and irresistible lease on life, spring is back in all her glory.

"The birds certainly know it. More and more, they whistle their happy tunes. Trees bud forth. Flowers begin to blossom once again. The whole land comes alive. Spring weaves her fascinating spell once more."

26. Interest area — business success
Type of speaker — a company owner, businessman or businesswoman, promotion director
Topic of speech — "The Ray Kroc Success Formula"
Partial introduction — "Ray Kroc, the founder of the McDonald's restaurant chain, is living proof that America is still a land of vast opportunity. Kroc's success formula in 1955 was the idea of licensing independent owners, thus creating the modern fast-food industry. Before he started his new business, Kroc was running a small Chicago firm that distributed a multimixer for malted milks. His sales ability, experience, and research enabled him to see a unique opportunity missed by so many others."

27. Interest area — personal advancement
Type of speaker — student, moonlighter, or anyone who believes in the entrepreneur spirit
Topic of speech — "Going to Work for Yourself"
Partial introduction — "The world of self-employment is wide open and offers you a variety of opportunities. A few of the many possibilities include mail-order, a typing, resume, or other service which you provide, and virtually any kind of business you offer for a fair price.

"The Small Business Administration says that there's one chance in five that a new business will still be operating and actually run by the same owner after a ten year period. The reason many businesses fail is a basic lack of business knowledge and ability. Ninety percent of the failures go under for lack of knowledge. But many small services you can run from your home don't take a lot of special knowledge. And you can start small and grow."

28. Interest area — religious growth
Type of speaker — church teacher, youth leader
Topic of speech — "Spiritual Treasures"
Partial introduction — "Many in today's world find it difficult to think about spiritual things. But the time and discipline spent on developing your spiritual life will pay real dividends both in this life and certainly in the life to come.

"There are material treasures and spiritual ones. We come into the world with nothing, and we will leave it with only what we've developed within ourselves spiritually. Some very wealthy persons find themselves haunted by the fact that they cannot take their wealth with them when their earthly lives are over."

29. Interest area — personal growth
Type of speaker — parent, teacher, club president, youth leader, counselor
Topic of speech — "Valuable Advice From a Boxing Immortal"
Partial introduction — "James Corbett was the first heavyweight in history to depend on his boxing skill and not sheer brute strength. Tall, clear-eyed, and an excellent boxer, he introduced the art of boxing to the rough and tumble brawls of the old days. He also left some valuable success advice for young and old in both his words and the example of his life."

Appendix I / Checklist for More Effective Speaking

The spotlight is really on you when your name is announced as the speaker for the evening, or luncheon, or whatever the occasion may be. This is the time when everything you've learned about public speaking is put to the test. It's your show.

I want to suggest some pointers that will upgrade your thinking about your speaking. Obviously, there are excellent, good, fair, and poor speech presentations given every day.

When I first began to speak to various audiences, I thought my basic style of presentation was good. Then one day, I tape-recorded it and disovered that my entire way of speaking (and the quality of it) could be greatly improved. I made up my mind then and there to streamline each speech I planned to give, to do my very best for each audience I addressed. After all, they were giving me their time and attention.

Being ready for each speech you present will certainly triple your chances for success. There's nothing like the confidence you'll feel when you know you're ready to inform, persuade, entertain, or inspire an audience. Here is a handy checklist to help you make sure that you're squared away before each speech:

1. Know the basic facts about your audience, their interest, age, education level, mutual goals, and more.
2. Get some ESP working for you before you speak to an au-

dience. By this, I mean visualize (in advance) your speech presentation. In your mind's eye, see your speech going well. See yourself going through the various sections of your speech, maintaining good eye contact, and doing an overall good job in communicating. Definitely see yourself handling any problems and not stumbling over your material, or getting notes lost, or whatever. Visualize a pleased and satisfied audience at the end of your speech.

3. Tape your entire speech one or more times *before* presentation. Listen to it critically and determine what needs to be done to upgrade and improve it. This comes under the step of practice. The more you've done to make your entire speech an effective one, the more confidence you'll have during the presentation.
4. Get to the place where your speech is to be given well ahead of the appointed time. Allow yourself extra time, in case you must drive across town. Unexpected things like flat tires, car trouble in general, weather storms, and just leaving too late can create havoc with your scheduled speech.
5. Thank your audience for the chance to speak to them. And also thank whoever introduces you as the speaker. You'd be surprised how many speakers forget to thank the person who introduces them.
6. Open your speech with a captivating attention-getter, if at all possible. If you don't grab attention right away, the rest of your speech could go down the tube.
7. Try to plan your speech (or much of it) around the self-interests of your audience (their jobs and careers, their homes and families, their health, and so on). The more your audience can identify with what your speech is all about, the better it will go over.
8. Pause occasionally in your presentation to see if what

you're saying is registering with your audience and if your listeners are still tuned in.

9. Use showmanship whenever possible in your speech presentations. In other words, do anything and everything you can to make your presentation sound attractive, bright, and interesting. It helps to think frequently about fresh and compelling ways to communicate the basic ideas and thoughts of your speech. Genuine showmanship is not trickery or deceit; it's a bright dynamic way to communicate something.
10. Don't try to continue your presentation if distractions take place (and keep on). If a fleet of ambulances or police cars converge in the area, you won't be able to compete with the noise level. Wait til the noise has ceased.
11. Maintain and continually add to a file of anecdotes, examples, and case histories. Such a file will prove to be invaluable when planning future speeches.
12. Time your speech when planning and practicing it. This way you'll know the length of the major sections, along with the total time needed to conclude your speech.
13. Decide at a fairly early point whether you intend to include a question-and-answer session in your speech presentation. Some speech topics lend themselves naturally to a question-and-answer period, following the conclusion of the speech. But you may not wish to open it up to questions from your audience. If you do include such a question period, be sure to figure the extra time needed. Keep in mind that many audiences like the chance to ask questions. Depending on the subject of your speech, these question periods can be quite popular and add to your total program's effectiveness.
14. Don't say everything on the same voice level. Get some variety in your voice. Let the power and force of your

voice come through at the right spots. Vary the loudness (not too loud) and lowness of your voice level. Do the same for your rate of delivery. Monotony can hurt any speech. Do your best to avoid it in your speeches.

15. Remember that the average person can retain a basic ABC explanation of something. But if your material gets too involved, complicated, or technical, you're going to lose a big chunk of your audience.
16. Know your speech presentation so well that you very rarely have to look away from your audience. This makes for much stronger communication.
17. Save some of the best or strongest material of your speech for the conclusion or last part. An ending that ties everything together nicely is well worth shooting for, as it leaves the audience with a satisfied feeling.
18. After you've been introduced and are making your way to the podium or lectern, be extra careful not to stumble. Some speakers have tripped and fallen over themselves just getting to the podium. It makes a bad impression on the audience. The audience is sizing you up in those first few minutes. First impressions count a great deal.
19. It's a good idea (and traditional with many speakers) to write the program chairman (or chairwoman, or whoever the spokesman was who invited you to speak) a note of thanks shortly after you've given the speech (say a week or so).
20. You might wish to ask for a letter of acknowledgment of the speech you gave (a letter stating that your speech was well received or to that effect). Once you have a number of such letters for the speeches you've presented, they can be of real help in lining up other speaking dates. They offer tangible proof that you can speak effectively before an audience.
21. If you wish to speak for other groups, let each one you *do*

speak for know of your interest in addressing other organizations, clubs, or groups. You can often get leads on other speaking dates in this way.

22. If you continue to enjoy public speaking, and after you've gained considerable experience and confidence in it, you may wish to learn more about the opportunities of the lecture circuit. Lecturing has, of course, become known as a wonderful sideline or moonlighting profession. George McGovern and Birch Bayh (as well as other well known people) speak several times a week at $2,500 to $3,000 per engagement. But unknown speakers are also doing well. Many of them are pulling down thousands of dollars and more every year for speaking engagements. They speak for business-professional organizations, college student groups, women's clubs, and associations.
23. Above all, keep growing and building confidence and skill as a public speaker. It will enrich your life and the lives of all the audiences you speak for. The speeches you present may well touch the lives of many people (especially over a long period of time) and help them to get more out of their years in any number of ways. More power to you as a public speaker!

Appendix II / A Self-Scoring Test on Speaking

Your answers to the following test questions will help you to determine which areas to work on to improve your speaking skills. Answer the questions with either a YES or NO and then refer to the directions on scoring your test:

1. Do you feel there's room for improvement in general as a speaker and communicator?
2. Are you willing to work on some weekends and weeknights, too, in order to advance as a speaker?
3. Do you think you would enjoy speaking to audiences more, if you could gain more experience at it?
4. Do you like to listen to well-known speakers who visit in your area to present speeches?
5. Do you accept any invitations to speak to various groups in your surrounding area?
6. When you achieve one of your goals, do you start moving forward toward the next one on your list?
7. Do you agree that the ability to speak well could add power and more success to your life?
8. Can you think of several subjects, which interest you as possible ideas for speeches?
9. Are you presently using all or most of your abilities and resources to get ahead?

10. Does the idea of speaking before a group of people interest you?
11. Do people sometimes tell you that you have a pleasant voice or that you would make a good speaker?
12. If it meant advancement and a higher income, would you be willing to travel around the country (and maybe overseas), in order to speak to various groups?
13. Are you sometimes inspired by a local, regional, or nationally prominent speaker?
14. Do you find yourself talking with your hands, when describing or narrating something to a friend?
15. Do you think it would be challenging or interesting to practice a speech presentation, by using a tape-recorder?
16. Do you feel it would be fun to be an after-dinner speaker, with the ability to amuse and entertain audiences?
17. Do you believe it would be worth the time and effort to develop a lecture program for presentation before a variety of audiences?
18. Does the idea or prospect of becoming a successful speaker on the profitable lecture circuit excite you?
19. Have you ever attended an all-day seminar of speeches by speakers who are authorities on certain subjects? (These seminars are frequently offered in many major cities.)
20. Do you think you might have something to contribute as a part-time speaker (and possibly a full-time speaker at some point in the future)?

See the following directions for scoring your answers.

How to Score Your Test Answers

Score *five* points for every YES answer and *zero* for each NO answer. Then add your total and place your score in this blank: ________.

TEST SCORING TABLE

Score	*Evaluation*
90 to 100	Excellent! Your high score shows you have a strong interest in public speaking. You could go far in the field, possibly, with this fine potential. You should think about becoming a professional speaker.
80 to 90	This is a good level of potential. It may be that you should consider getting into public speaking, as a part-time sideline. The seeds of success are there.
70 to 80	You've got a fair degree of interest in the speaking-communication field. While you are somewhat limited in what you might achieve, you might be able to develop from this point.
Under 70	Based on this score, you don't have enough interest or motivation.

Index